S0-BYA-511

JOURNEY TO UPOLU

JOURNEY

ROBERT LOUIS STEVENSON,

ALSO BY EDWARD RICE

MOTHER INDIA'S CHILDREN

THE MAN IN THE SYCAMORE TREE

TEMPLE OF THE PHALLIC KING

THE GANGES

TO UPOLU

VICTORIAN REBEL

EDWARD RICE

DODD, MEAD & COMPANY · NEW YORK

The photographs on the following pages are from the Stevenson Collection in the Beinecke Rare Book and Manuscript Library, Yale University: pages 5, 10, 13, 19, 32, 38, 40, 43, 47, 54, 67, 83, 97, 100, 102, 106, 109, 112, 118, 119, 122, 123, 124, 125, 132, 139, 141, 143, 144.

The photograph on the following page is from the Taft Museum: page 96.

Copyright © 1974 by Edward Rice
All rights reserved
No part of this book may be reproduced in any form
without permission in writing from the publisher

ISBN: 0-396-06933-9
Library of Congress Catalog Card Number: 73-21164
Printed in the United States of America

CONTENTS

INTRODUCTION

THIS is a book about two people and a family, for any biography of Robert Louis Stevenson is also a biography of his wife, Fanny Van der Grift Osbourne, and, as well, of her children Lloyd and Belle.

Stevenson was born Robert Lewis Balfour Stevenson. At eighteen he changed the Lewis to Louis, though it was still pronounced in the Scots way, and dropped the Balfour. His wife, an American, as English biographers like to point out, called him Lou-us. Fanny, born Frances Matilda Vandergrift, changed the spelling of her surname to the earlier Van der Grift when she ran away from her husband, Sam Osbourne, and went to Europe to study art. Stevenson occasionally called her "the Vandergrifter." Fanny's older son, who plays an important role in the family group and collaborated with Stevenson on several novels, was known as Sam or Sammy or Sammy Lloyd until he was in his late teens, and then as Lloyd. So much for the changes of names. We will use the better known versions, even when anachronistic.

These are frontier people, Stevenson and Fanny. In Stevenson's case the frontier was physical, literary, psychological. He defied conventions and authority, took unpopular stands. Many of his uncomfortably outspoken opinions were ignored by relatives, friends and the public on the theory that they were merely passing whims. But they weren't. As a young man he spoke out on the hypocrisy of nineteenth-century sexual relationships and religious beliefs; then on his own guilt for being a member of the privileged classes. He made unequivocal statements about race and skin color, statements that were ignored at the time, and even have little place in the "enlightened" biographies of this century. He opposed Western imperialism in the Pacific, but his friends and his readers dismissed his warnings. His stand against the white colonials and in favor of the Samoans nearly resulted in his deportation from the island of Samoa.

He married a divorced, older woman despite the almost complete disapproval of his family and friends. His wife was most likely partly black; few, if any, of Stevenson's friends took kindly to her. He expressed some "socialistic" points of view on certain issues; he advocated the end of the death penalty; in the South Pacific he "went native" in the eyes of the other Europeans. Virtually everything he did was on the edge of a frontier, even his choice of occupation as a writer, for no gentleman ever "scribbled." He roamed the frontiers of the Victorian age, and spent the last years of his life in the vast, poorly charted frontier of the South Pacific, still undeveloped, primitive, "savage" at the time of his death.

His wife, Fanny, was a child of the true frontier, being raised in the town of Indianapolis when it was hardly more than twenty years old and had a population of only three thousand people. She spent the first years of her married life to Sam Osbourne in Nevada mining camps, and then in the frontier state of California. She had the courage to run away from her faithless husband, and then to seek a divorce despite the stigma it cast on a woman in her century.

Stevenson and Fanny were wanderers—restless, eager, curious, friendly, hard-working. They endured hardship that would have dispirited and stopped many other people. Stevenson's literary production, produced under extremely difficult conditions, was the equivalent of several other writers. And both Stevenson and Fanny were sickly, Stevenson experiencing regular hemorrhaging of the lungs throughout most of his life. Fanny suffered from gallstones, among other ailments (some of which were likely psychosomatic but nevertheless painful), and underwent an exploratory operation for cancer of the throat. She alternated between an explosive energy and the sickbed. Her son, Lloyd, was also not spared. As a young man he was expected to go blind, and he prepared himself for the tragedy. Yet, despite the constant cry of anguish that arose in their private correspondence and in their conversations with friends (to the extent that the Stevensons earned an unfortunate "cry wolf" reputation—they did not quite expire when they said they would after pleading ill health and grinding poverty), their public stance, and his writings, radiated only the most blatant cheerfulness and optimism.

It is interesting to see how the early biographies, including the more or less "official" works about Stevenson and Fanny by either relatives or close friends, presented sanctimonious and censored views of the writer and his wife, eliminating unfavorable material, opinions, acts and incidents. Stevenson passed his teens, his twenties and early thirties in extreme poverty, even though his family was well off. This was because he wanted to be a writer and not an engineer as his father wished, and had to survive on a meagre allowance and low payments for his articles and books. His very interesting account of his trip to America by emigrant ship was bought back from the publisher by his father, along with some other material the older Stevenson didn't want the public to know about; even when the text was finally released after Stevenson's death, it was heavily censored so that the reader would not know the frightful conditions under which young Stevenson traveled. Many of his poems dealing with amorous or "sexual" themes were withheld by his widow, and their discovery and eventual publication came about largely by chance.

His manuscripts were discussed by Fanny Stevenson and his friends while he worked on them; their criticisms often reached the point of censorship or an attempt to force him into telling a story according to their views, not his. His letters were released in a heavily edited version, the first collection by Sidney Colvin, a man who, as we will see, had special reason to censor many of them. All of these changes, acts of censorship and bowdlerizing, editing and postmortem rewriting helped contribute to the image of Stevenson as a "seraph in chocolate," in the phrase of one of his friends, Henley, who violently attacked the official biography prepared by Stevenson's cousin Graham Balfour. It wasn't until much later, in the 1920's, that "another" Stevenson began to emerge. Some of the corrective views are as extreme as the censored ones, and it behooves any current biographer to steer a careful course between the two aspects of his subject.

In preparing his biography I have taken a fresh look at certain of the original texts. Stevenson's views on many subjects were startlingly contemporary to our times. He was interested in race problems (the Chinese, American Indians and the peoples of the Pacific, for example); he was outspoken on the sexual hypocrisy among his peers in Victorian Scotland and England; he took a strong stand against colonialism and the exploitation of indigenous people. He would never have thought of himself as a social anthropologist, yet many of his writings on the South Pacific—now ignored as dull and trivial—are as sharply observant and much more graphic than works by our contemporary sociologists and anthropologists. He did not write about cross-cousin relationships and other anthropological minutiae, but his observations—and understanding—of a subject such as cannibalism shows that he was a man who could to some extent put himself into the mind and psyche of a preliterate islander. He matured as he wrote: his early writings are highly mannered, even arch, and shallow, but he passed a kind of watershed in his first trip to America, and his later works are more mature, better, deeper.

Like many people of my own generation I was brought up on Stevenson. I can remember *A Child's Garden of Verses* being read to me when I was very young and ill in bed. Then I read *Treasure Island* over and over, and *Kidnapped, David Balfour, The Strange Case of Dr. Jekyll and Mr. Hyde, The Suicide Club* and many other of Stevenson's romantic and popular works. Stevenson seemed to die out as a popular author, though I read *Treasure Island* to my own children one summer when we were abroad on a trip and had some long hours to pass. He seemed to have drifted away, a minor author. It wasn't until I was preparing for an expedition of my own to the South Pacific that I recalled that Stevenson had been there. I began to read Stevenson on the South Pacific, and then some of his other works, and I finally realized that Stevenson was not only a man of his age but of ours. And when I was working on this biography, when I would mention it to my own contemporaries, it was as if I said some secret password. Stevenson! A whole new world comes roaring forward in this stoop-shouldered, coughing adventurer who came to America in the hold of an immigrant ship and died a Samoan chief.

A detail from the large medallion done by the American sculptor, Augustus Saint-Gaudens when Stevenson arrived in New York on his second, triumphant visit. Stevenson was sitting in bed, smoking and writing, while Saint-Gaudens made the sketches. There are several versions of the medallion; in some the cigarette has been changed to a pen.

JOURNEY TO UPOLU

A CHILD ALONE

To start at the simple beginnings: Robert Louis (or Robert Lewis Balfour) Stevenson was born on 13 November, 1850, in Edinburgh, Scotland, to upper-middle-class parents. The Stevensons (father, uncle, grandfather) were engineers distinguished in lighthouse building along Scotland's rugged coastline. As for parental influence, Stevenson's father, Thomas, is said to have been one of those men who felt a duty to mankind by inventing the revolving light, but refused to patent it and thereby profit from saving lives. He is described as "stern, chivalrous, puritanical, melancholy, upright." After his father's death, Stevenson wrote that "He was a man of somewhat antique strain, with a blended sternness and softness that was wholly Scottish, and at first somewhat bewildering; with a profound, essential melancholy of disposition and (what oftens accompanies it) the most humorous geniality in company; shrewd and childish; passionately attached, passionately prejudiced; a man of many extremes, many faults of temper, and no very stable foothold for himself among life's troubles. Yet he was a wise adviser; many men, and these not inconsiderable, took counsel with him habitually."

Stevenson's mother, Margaret, was tall, slim, fair, practical and humorous. She kept a daily journal of her son's life, hardly missing a single entry. The woman who served as Stevenson's nurse, Alison Cunningham, otherwise known as Cummy, had an influence on him as strong as his parents, perhaps even stronger and more pronounced. Stevenson retained her friendship until his death.

As a child Stevenson was very delicate and was ill much of the time. For most winters of his early years he spent long periods in bed. Edinburgh in the winter is extremely damp, raw and blustery. In writing about the city of his birth and his childhood, Stevenson said: "Many winters I never crossed the threshold, but used to lie on my face in the nursery floor, chalking or painting in watercolours the pictures in the illustrated papers; or sit up in bed with a little shawl pinned about my shoulders, to play with bricks or whatnot."

✻

It is a common, tragic Victorian picture, virtually a cliché: a small boy, constantly ill, in bed with his toys; a warm, motherly woman, his nanny Cummy, fussing over him, reading to him, taking care of him. "How well I remember her lifting me out of bed, carrying me to the window and showing me one or two lit windows up in Queen Street, across the dark belt of gardens, where also, we told each other, there might be sick little boys and their nurses waiting, like us, for the morning.

Years later he described some of the tortured nights, writing about himself in the third person: "He was from a child an ardent and uncomfortable dreamer. When he had a touch of fever at night, and the room swelled and shrank, and his clothes, hanging on a nail, now loomed up instant to the bigness of a church, and now drew away into a horror of infinite distance and infinite littleness, the poor soul was very well aware of what must follow, and struggled hard against the approaches of that slumber which was the beginning of sorrows. But his struggles were in vain; sooner or later the night-hag would have him by the throat, and pluck him, strangling and screaming, from his sleep. His dreams were at times commonplace enough, at times very strange: at times they were almost formless, he would be haunted, for instance, by nothing more definite than a certain hue of brown, which he did not mind in the least while he was awake, but feared and loathed while he was dreaming; at times, again, they took on every detail of circumstance, as when once he supposed he must swallow the popular world, and awoke screaming with the horror of the thought. The two chief troubles of his very narrow existence—the practical and everyday trouble of school tasks and the ultimate and airy one of hell and judgment—were often confounded together into one appalling nightmare. He seemed to himself to stand before the Great White Throne; he was called on, poor little devil, to recite some form of words, on which his destiny depended; his tongue stuck, his memory was blank, hell gaped for him; and he would awake, clinging to the curtain-rod with his knees to his chin."

As he grew older the nightmares lessened, thought still "for the most part miserable." "He would awake with no more extreme symptom than a flying heart, a freezing scalp, cold sweats, and the speechless midnight fear."

Lonely child, ill, nurse fussing over him. Long days in bed. Mother and Cummy bringing warm soups, tempting dishes. The boy doesn't eat. The city is raw, blustery, damp; the chill gnaws ones bones.

> Close by the jolly fire I sit
> To warm my frozen bones a bit.

To detail the events of his childhood is unnecessary. His early years are both lonely and warm, instructive to the reader and Victorian in the worst sense. What stands out most is the subject matter the analyst likes to play with—which is not the purpose of this biography, however. That Stevenson was close to two older, warm, motherly women—his two mothers—was lonely, imaginative, self-entertaining, is obvious. Later in life he was definitely attracted to women older than himself, but the theories have no great relevance in the light of the fact that Stevenson, an unusual man, met an unusual woman and together they led an unusual life in an unusual part of the world. Which is what this book is about.

Cummy was only a young woman barely out of the countryside when she came to the Stevenson household. The boy she was to care for was just eighteen months old when she arrived. She was not only his nurse and second—perhaps "first"—mother, but his primary source of information about the world. It was through her close association that he gained much of his knowledge, and about his Scottish past and daily events in the outside world. Cummy was not only a great source of Scottish legend, myth and folklore but a careful reader of the popular press. Through her Stevenson learned of the robberies, murders, the great crimes that took place in Edinburgh and London and other great cities.

Stevenson's dedication of *A Child's Garden of Verses* states quite unequivocally his feelings about Cummy, for he calls her "My second Mother, my first Wife,/ the angel of my infant life——" and also speaks of "the long nights you lay awake/And watched for my unworthy sake."

Cummy was a deeply convinced Scotch Presbyterian, and from her, as from his parents, Stevenson was subjected to a heavy indoctrination of Calvinist theology and beliefs, which weighed so heavy upon him that in his late teens he began to reject it.

The eight-year-old Stevenson (at the right), with his cousin Bob. At the time young Stevenson was nicknamed "Smout," the term for trout fry.

✺

Before Stevenson learned to write, he would make up verses and stories, which Cummy wrote down for him. "I thought they were rare nonsense," she said later. His mother kept a diary of his life, writing down the daily events and saving every picture he drew and every line he dictated or wrote.

A turning point in the young author's life: his Uncle David offers a Bible picture book to the one among his countless nephews and nieces who can write the best history of Moses. Still unable to write, young Stevenson, age six, dictates the story to his mother and illustrates it with his own drawings. First prize for the young author. His mother: "It was [now] the desire of his heart to be an author."

He has few friends because of his health. The child is not allowed to run, play, roughhouse with his contemporaries. Shortly after Stevenson's sixth birthday his cousin Bob (Robert Alan Mowbray Stevenson) visits him for the winter. Bob is three and a half years older but finds Louis a delightful companion. The two boys have toy theatres, soldiers, play war. One of their chief delights: "Rival kingdoms of our own invention—Nosingham and Encyclopedia, of which we were perpetually drawing maps." There is a traumatic wrench in young Stevenson's life when he is eight: Bob, and his sister Katharine, also close to Stevenson, are suddenly taken away. Their father, an engineer and lighthouse builder in the family tradition, has a "nervous breakdown." The family goes abroad.

Stevenson's life becomes more open. Short trips to the countryside near Edinburgh. An attempt at school, which is abandoned. He does not return to formal schooling until he is nine.

✿

Traumatizing figure in the background: Grandfather Balfour. "We children admired him, partly for his beautiful face and silver hair . . . partly for the solemn light in which we beheld him once a week, the observed of all observers, in the pulpit. But his strictness and distance, the effect, I now fancy, of old age, slow blood, and settled habit, oppressed us with a kind of terror. When not abroad, he sat much alone, writing sermons or letters to his scattered family in a dark and cold room with a library of bloodless books." Grandfather Balfour's study is decorated with many Indian pictures, in bright colors and dear to young eyes ("the redeeming grace"). "When I was once sent in to say a psalm to my grandfather, I went, quaking indeed with fear, but at the same time glowing with hope that, if I said it well, he might reward me with an Indian picture." The psalm, well said, brings no picture, and not even a sugar candy, one of which Grandfather Balfour eats before the young Stevenson.

School begins for Stevenson in 1859, but his formal education is constantly interrupted by illness, travel and change of institutions. He is constantly at home with colds and other sicknesses, forerunner of the chronic lung illness that was to be his constant companion. His father, lenient in the matter of education, did not believe in forcing a child to study, so Stevenson wandered through school attending classes where he cared to (Latin, French and mathematics).

His reading at the time: *Robinson Crusoe* and *Swiss Family Robinson* ("that dreary family," he wrote later), a book called *Paul Blake* and some of the works of Mayne Reid. He also reads, finding on the austere shelves of his father's library the proceedings of learned societies (physical science, optics) and cyclopedias; *Rob Roy, Guy Mannering, Pilgrim's Progress, Voyages of Captain Woods Rogers,* Ainsworth's *Tower of London,* four old bound volumes of *Punch.* He is constantly interested in writing, and writes all the time—"scribble" is the word many of his biographers use—stories of violent adventure, one teenage work being subtitled "Adventures in the South Seas"; it is about two midshipmen who are wrecked, captured by savage islanders and almost burned alive.

At thirteen his health improves and he begins to play with his contemporaries. One of them (unknown) later describes him at the time: "A slender, long-legged boy in pepper and salt tweeds, with an undescribable influence that forced us to include him in our play as a looker-on, critic and slave driver. . . . No one had the remotest intention of competing with R.L.S. in story making, and his tales, had we known it, were such as the world would listen to in silence and wonder." Stevenson is the initiator in beginning magazines at school and at home, which are circulated among his companions. One was *The Sun-*

Stevenson's father, Thomas Stevenson, the
dour, capable engineer and lighthouse builder.

beam Magazine, another *The School Boy Magazine*, an illustrated (in color) miscellany of "fact, fiction and fun." The latter had four serial stories. He also began a number of short stories and novels, most of which have been destroyed. One of the few surviving works is a small pamphlet of twenty pages called "The Pentland Rising, a page of history, 1666," which drew its inspiration from Cummy's anecdotes about Scottish history, and which his father had printed.

Meanwhile, with his parents he makes his first trip abroad. He is twelve. The family first visits London and the English countryside; then they go to Hamburg in Germany. Later in the year comes a trip to southern France, taking with them a niece, staying in a town called Mentone for two months. In March the Stevensons make a tour of Italy, returning home via Austria and the Rhine River. This is the beginning of regular trips to France for young Stevenson; he goes again to Mentone in the winter of the next year with his mother, remaining on the Riviera until the following May. The two succeeding years bring spring trips to France again, but after that he must wait several years, and for different circumstances, before he goes abroad again.

His cousin, Graham Balfour, said that, "The curious point about the foreign journeys is that they seemed to have little manifest influence upon Stevenson, and to have passed almost entirely out of his life." Yet, in Mentone, Stevenson learns French, picking it up so quickly and colloquially that his teacher soon drops formal lessons and prefers to pass the time in conversation with this most unusual youngster. However, a young cousin who went along on the first trip of 1863 remarked on how much Stevenson developed during this period. "In some ways he was more like a boy of sixteen," she wrote. His father was a great believer in the virtues of traveling, and took his son with him on an adult basis. She says: "In the hotel at Nice he began to take Louis to the smoking room with him; there my uncle was always surrounded by a group of eager and amused listeners—English, American, Russian—and every subject, political, artistic and theological, was discussed and argued. Uncle Tom's genial manner found friends wherever he went, and the same sort of thing went on during the whole journey."

Yet this highly sensitive teenager is looking for more than scenery and conversations in smoking rooms. Balfour cryptically remarks: "Of the other side of his character, of the solitary, dreamy, rather unhappy child, but little record survives, or little evidence which can be assigned with certainty to these years." But he was unhappy; one of his letters to his mother, written when he was thirteen, was so miserable in its content that she burned it.

He knew all along that he wanted to do nothing but write. Finally he is allowed to fix up a room on the top floor of their house as a study

Stevenson's mother, Margaret, whom he resembled more than his father.

and writing room, and here he spends hours at work on stories or writing out in the best manner possible things and scenes and events that have impressed him. He is highly critical of himself: "I liked doing them indeed, but when I was done I could see they were rubbish."

Different plans are afoot for young Stevenson. In that age young people followed, as much as possible, certain prescribed routes. The young had a voice only to say Yes. One normally followed the trade or profession or career of the family, or of one's father. Farmers begat farmers, tradesmen begat tradesmen, engineers begat engineers. Stevenson, it was clear in his father's eyes, was to be the sixth member of his family to hold a place on the Board of Northern Lights. What could be more solid, more enduring, than the career of engineer, directing the solid, substantial family firm in its service to mankind?

Into the University of Edinburgh he goes, to study engineering, with little heart for the grinding hours before him. Lighthouses beckon! Three and a half years they are to consume of his life, this fruitless pursuit of a degree in science. Yet the work has its pleasanter moments. In the summer of 1868, Stevenson, almost eighteen, joins an engineering party at Anstruther, on the Scottish coast, where a breakwater is under construction. Here he has his first opportunity of seeing engineering in the field—rough, wet work, but he enjoys it. Then he spends three weeks on the once-deserted Earraid Island off Mull, which leaves such an impression on his memory that years later he employs it as the site of David Balfour's shipwreck in *Kidnapped*.

He descends in the heavy, weighted diver's dress to the foundation of the breakwater they are building. It was an interesting period for him, and what he was learning seemed worthwhile.

"What I gleaned I am sure I do not know, but indeed I had already my own private determination to be an author . . . though I haunted the breakwater by day, and even loved the place for the sake of the sunshine, the thrilling sea-side air, the wash of the waves on the sea face, the green glimmer of the diver's helmets far below." But, as he adds: "My own genuine occupation lay elsewhere and my only industry was the hours when I was not on duty." As soon as his dinner was finished (he was lodging with a carpenter named Bailie Brown), he drew his "chair to the table" and "proceeded to pour forth literature."

Yet, wrote Stevenson, "I wish to speak with sympathy of my education as an engineer. It takes a man into the open air; keeps him hanging about harbor sides, the richest form of idling; it carries him to wild islands; it gives him a taste of the genial danger of the sea. . . . From the roaring skerry and the wet thwart of the tossing boat, he passes to stool and desk, and with a memory full of ships and seas and perilous headlands and shining pharos, he must apply his long-sighted eyes to the pretty niceties of drawing or measure his inaccurate mind with several pages of consecutive figures."

Much as he enjoyed the outdoor work, he could not apply himself to his engineering studies, and his university record was abysmally poor. "No one ever played truant with more deliberate care and no one ever had more certificates for less education."

Alison Cunningham, whom young Stevenson called "Cummy."
She was not only his nurse but his eyes on the outside world.

VELVET COAT

THOUGH he had been a sickly child, he was—so his mother and Cummy said—a frank and happy one. But he grew progressively more unhappy in his teens, and now at the University he is lonely and moody, and avoids the social life that his family's position affords. He shuns dinners and parties if he can. He reads a lot, Shakespeare and Alexandre Dumas being particular favorites. By now the family has acquired a country house, Swanston Cottage, in the Pentland Hills overlooking Edinburgh. Here Stevenson spends much of his time roaming the countryside and, with his amazing knack of using every sight and sound, storing the memories for later use in his writings, many of which are drawn upon the area around Swanston, notably his fine novel *St. Ives*, which he was to write years later in Samoa. He talks to the local farmers and shepherds, whose exploits in driving sheep into England along side roads and hill paths resembled those of the American cattlemen on their long treks.

Despite his unhappiness over his studies, the University offers opportunities he hadn't dreamed of. His horizons widen; he begins to question the middle-class life he has been raised in, and above all, he now seriously challenges the religious doctrines instilled in him since infancy. His childhood had been restricted, conventional, tightly Calvinistic Presbyterian. He rebelled, becoming an atheist, challenging his father, pouring out ideas in a flood, waving his arms, pacing the floor as he talked. Shocking! In a letter to his cousin Katharine, Bob's younger sister, he uses the phrase, "God, if there is such a gentleman—" The climax will come at twenty-three when he writes his father a letter detailing his atheistic concepts.

He scares some people with his wildness, his movements, his appearance, though others say he is merely showing off. He dresses oddly, "continental" style in a velvet jacket; he wears his hair long. He is outspoken on Christian hypocrisy. "Pray, what was Christ, if you be Christian?" he asks in a poem addressed to the self-satisfied citizens of Edinburgh.

> O fine, religious decent folk
> In Virtue's flaunting gold and scarlet,
> I sneer between two puffs of smoke—
> Give me the publican and harlot.
>
> .   .   .   .   .
>
> If Christ were only here just now
> Among the city's wynds and gables
> Teaching the life he taught us, how
> Would he be welcome to your tables?

He suffers guilt over his favored life. In an essay about a young man, who is obviously none other than himself ("with some high notions, and on the search for higher thoughts of life"), he outlines the dilemma that has developed: "He got hold of some unsettling works, the New Testament among others, and this loosened his views of life and led him into many perplexities. As he was the son of a man in a certain position, and well off, my friend had enjoyed from the first the advantages of education, nay, he had been kept alive through a sickly childhood by constant watchfulness, comforts, and change of air, for all of which he was indebted to his father's wealth.

"At college he met other lads more dilgent than himself, who followed the plough in summer-time to pay their fees in winter; and this inequality struck him with some force. He was at that age of a conversible temper, and insatiably curious in the aspects of life; and he spent much of his time scraping acquaintance with all classes of man- and woman-kind. In this way he came upon many depressed ambitions and intelligences stunted for want of opportunity; and this also struck him. He began to perceive that life was a handicap upon strange, wrong-sided principles; and not, as he had been told, a fair and equal race. He began to tremble that he himself had been unjustly favoured, when he saw all the avenues of wealth, and power, and comfort closed against so many of his competitors and equals, and held unwearingly open before so idle, desultory, and so dissolute a being as himself."

The solution, which he was soon to follow, was a virtually complete rejection of his advantages. But at the same time he was hopelessly entangled in the upper-middle-class life that he was incapable of doing other than relying upon, year after year, until he was thirty-seven. What he wanted was this: "Once he put on his boots," he writes, still speaking of himself in the third person, "like any other unripe donkey, to run away from home, it was his best consolation that he was now, at a single plunge, to free himself from the responsibility of this wealth that was not his, and to do battle equally against his fellows in the warfare of life." He was to do such a battle, but under such a handicap one wonders how he survived. Only a man of unimaginable inner toughness could have lived as Stevenson was to live.

Meanwhile, until he is twenty-three, his father gives him an allowance of five shillings a week, the equivalent of a few dollars in our purchasing power. "The result," says Balfour, "was that the lad went his own way, and frequented places which consorted with his means." A Victorian euphemism, for Stevenson is now passing his time in such places as The Green Elephant, The Twinkling Eye and the Gay Japanese. Bars and brothels, that is. "I was always kept poor in my youth, to my great indignation at the time," writes Stevenson, "but since then with my complete approval." His experiences and the environment formed the background for certain works later on. 'Twelve pounds a year was my allowance up to twenty-three," and he adds, "which was indeed far too little." Then: "Looking back upon it, I am surprised at the courage with which I first ventured alone into the societies in which I moved; I was the companion of seamen, chimney-sweeps, and thieves; my circle was continually being changed by the action of the police magistrate. . . . I was distinctly petted and respected [he doesn't say where, but obviously in the city's brothels]; the women were most gentle and kind to me. . . . Such indeed was my celebrity [he was known as Velvet Coat] that when the proprietor and his mistress came to inspect the establishment, I was invited to tea with them." He was always a most sensitive and compasionate person, for: "It is still a grisly thought to me, that I have since seen that mistress, then gorgeous in velvet and gold chains, an old, toothless, ragged woman, with hardly enough voice to welcome me by my old name of Velvet Coat."

Stevenson's sexual interests were usually concealed by euphemisms or ignored completely by his biographers; in general they were passed off as youthful "hot-bloodedness." It was not until some thirty years after his death, in the enlightened 1920's, that a biographer was able to say that "Stevenson's dissipation was really a byword in the decorous society of Edinburgh," without even then being explicit. It was one of the clichés of the nineteenth and early twentieth centuries

that university students were expected to act in certain socially tolerated but officially deplored ways—to "sow their wild oats," in the
hackneyed phrase of the past. It was understood in Victorian Britain
that young men of better families would patronize low saloons and
brothels, which is what Stevenson did. He never denied his youthful
sexual drives, and sex hypocrisy was a theme he treated in his poetry
not only then but in his later years. He immersed himself in the flesh-
pots of Edinburgh. A fine situation for a fine young man from a fine
family! But wild oats are a passing phase for most young men, who
afterwards marry nice young ladies whom their families have virtually
selected, or at least passed upon. A "more than ordinary sexual drive"
would be a simple way of expressing this aspect of Stevenson's coming
of age in a rigorous, Calvinistic milieu. Stevenson pushed the recognized boundaries to the limit and beyond, as he was to do in many
other areas. And he was to marry outside his milieu, defying family
and convention.

✿

A day of reckoning: Stevenson passes his time at the University,
knowing he is failing his studies and that nothing will come of a career
in engineering. The Board of Northern Lights, devoted to illuminating
the treacherous seas, is never to gain a most luminous member.
Thomas Stevenson is finally aware of the low grades and calls in his
son. "One dreadful day . . ." is how the younger Stevenson describes it.
Thomas Stevenson takes his errant, slightly ridiculous misfit son on a
fatherly stroll to discuss the situation. Stevenson tells his father he is
interested in nothing but writing. A ridiculous statement, for everyone
knows that writing—that is, "scribbling"—is a pastime, not a profession. The great writers of the age are all gentlemen, or are gentle-
manly employed and scribble in their free time. Lord So and So and
Sir This and That. Etcetera.

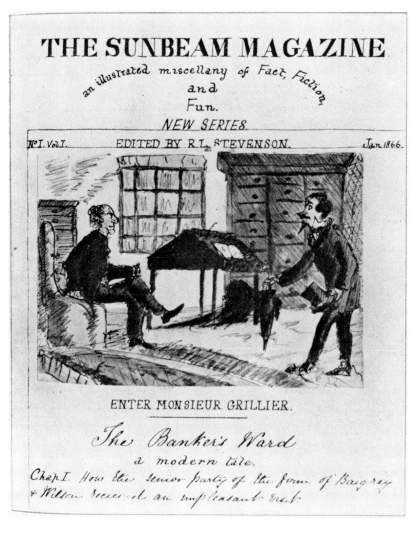

THE SUNBEAM MAGAZINE

an illustrated miscellany of Fact, Fiction

and

Fun.

NEW SERIES.

No. I. Vol. I.   EDITED BY R.L. STEVENSON.   Jan 1866.

ENTER MONSIEUR GRILLIER.

The Banker's Ward

a modern tale.

Chap I. How the senior party of the firm of Baigrey
& Wilson received an unpleasant visit.

The first issue of The Sunbeam Magazine, *one of several pub-*
lications Stevenson edited and published during his teens.

What controlled anger must have burned in Thomas Stevenson's
rent heart, enough to light all of the coast! Bitterness, disappointment,
fury carefully bounded by his dour heart. He is able to suggest . . . a
compromise: Stevenson is to take up the study of law, which will give

him a solidly-based, respectable profession and, if that is his wish, time for scribbling. At least the family's reputation will be protected. Will parents never learn?

Dutifully Stevenson begins his lectures in law.

A past biographer, covering up much of what is embarrassing or difficult, writes that "in spite of the fact that his law studies now left him with the opportunity for the work he wanted so much to do, Louis was far from happy." And despite the compromise the father is bitterly disappointed at the course of events, for not only does he see the family firm ending, he also believes that his son is, in the parlance of the times, an "idler," which means that he is not truly engaged in any active productive work, is not looking forward to a solid Scottish mansion and family, is not planning on carrying on the family profession, and what is more, dresses slovenly and is sowing too many wild oats. And his religious opinions!

The conflict is basic, and despite the attempts of Stevenson's friends to pretend later on that father and son actually were close, the gulf for a long time is unbridgeable. In fact, it takes an epic proportion in a dream of Freudian classicality that Stevenson had. When he wrote it out he did not give the general date, as he did of certain other dreams. He speaks in the third person, and then says of the dreamer, "He is no less a person than myself." The dream is this:

The dreamer is "the son of a very rich and wicked man, the owner of broad acres and a most damnable temper." The son, to avoid his father, "lived very much abroad." The son returns to England to find his father married to a young wife who suffers cruelly and hates her situation. Father and son want to meet each other, but since neither will go to the other, they meet in a desolate, sandy country by the sea; here they quarrel. The son, "stung by some intolerable insult, struck down the father dead."

The father's body is found but no murder is suspected. The son inherits his father's estate and now lives under the same roof as the widow. The two grow "daily better friends," but it suddenly occurs to the young man that his stepmother has conceived an idea of his guilt. He withdraws from her company "as men draw back from a precipice suddenly discovered," yet the old intimacy is renewed again and again, only to be broken each time. They live "at cross purposes, a life full of broken dialogue, challenging glances, and supressed passion."

One day the woman slips away from the house. The son follows her. She goes to the lonely beach, finds a bit of evidence the dreamer cannot recall upon awakening. She slips, hangs in peril from the dunes' sand-wreaths. The son leaps forward to rescue her. She is about to explain herself, but he cuts her short with a trivial remark, and arm in arm they return to the railway station. Later he searches her room for the bit of evidence she has found. The woman appears; she tries to speak but again he cuts her off. The next morning they breakfast together; she makes sly allusions to the situation. He leaps to his feet, asking again and again, Why did she torture him? She too leaps to her feet, pale-faced, then falls on her knees. "Do you not understand," she cries, "I love you!"

This, in brief, is a summary of Stevenson's dilemma: the conflict with his father, living off his wealth, wishing subconsciously to get him out of the way, and loving his father's wife, in real life his own mother. Or does the young wife represent Cummy? Probably Stevenson was oblivious to the psychological content of the dream when he wrote it out for the benefit of the public—techniques of dream analysis in psychological terms had not been discovered by Sigmund Freud. Yet it is a most revealing commentary on his inner and mundane lives, as are some of the other dreams in his essay, "A Chapter on Dreams."

Stevenson ascribed his dreaming to "the Little People," who put things into his sleeping mind. He said they gave him a number of ideas for stories, including the plot of *The Strange Case of Dr. Jekyll and Mr. Hyde.* Yet Stevenson had some suspicion that dreams were intimately connected with waking life, for he began his essay by writing, "The past is all of one texture—whether feigned or suffered—whether acted out in three dimensions, or only witnessed into that small theatre of the brain which we keep brightly lighted all night long, after the jets are down, and darkness and sleep reign undisturbed in the remainder of the body."

✽

He would have liked to write out the dream as a story, but "it soon became plain that in this spirited tale there were unmarketable elements."

✽

He joins the University Conservative Club, though he is a "Socialist" of the nineteenth-century type, a non-Marxian, and he is elected to the Speculative Society early in 1869. The Society was a singular honor, for it had only thirty members; at a meeting one of the members would read an essay, which would then be debated. Stevenson was likely to talk about literary subjects. In one meeting he moved that the nineteenth-century revival of letters was declining; in another he supported the view that American literature could compare favorably with the contemporaneous literature of England. These are rather trivial subjects. A major issue was a debate on the death penalty, in March, 1870, in which Stevenson stood alone in advocating its end. The question had been: "Is the Abolition of Capital Punishment desirable?" Graham Balfour writes: "If he ever held the opinion, it certainly found no favour with him in after life," a most questionable assertion, for in the pages of his last—unfinished—novel, *Weir of Hermiston,* Stevenson returns to the issue. Here Archie, the son of the notorious, brutal, gross and inhuman Lord Justice-Clerk, protests an

Stevenson as a student.

instance of the death penalty imposed by his father. Twenty-four years after he himself had objected to the death penalty, and in this book that echoes his conflict with his own father, Stevenson tries to put both the question of capital punishment and duty to the man who begat the son into focus. Archie sees the trial of one Duncan Jopp, a cowardly, vice-ridden creature, who nevertheless "was still a man, and had eyes and apprehension." Archie's father, the judge, "did not affect the virtue of impartiality; this was no case for refinement; there was a man to be hanged." So the judge sentences Jopp to death. "The judge had pursued him with a monstrous, relishing gaiety, horrible to be conceived, a trait for night-mares. It is one thing to spear a tiger, another to crush a toad."

Then Archie goes to the place of execution. "He saw the fleering rabble, the flinching wretch produced. He looked on for a while at a certain parody of devotion, which seemed to strip the wretch of his last claim to manhood. Then followed the brutal instant of extinction, and the paltry dangling of the remains like a broken jumping-jack. He had been prepared for something terrible, not for this tragic meanness. He stood a moment silent, and then—'I denounce this God-defying murder' he shouted." At a meeting of the Speculative Society that evening, Archie proposes that the next debate be: "Whether capital punishment be consistent with God's will or man's policy?" The result among his fellow members is "a breath of embarrassment, of something like alarm." The subject is not seconded. After the meeting, "Archie found himself alone." His father hears about his protest at the execution and his attempt to debate the subject at the Society, and confronts him in a long, relentless meeting that wears down the son. "Father, it was a hideous thing," says Archie. "Grant he was vile, why should you hunt him with a vileness equal to his own? It was done with glee—that is the word—you did it with glee; and I looked on, God help me! with horror."

But the judge keeps after Archie, and finally Archie, "aware of some illogicality in his position"—though Stevenson does not define it, finally cannot be but abject and apologetic. He asks his father's pardon. One feels that Archie gives in not to the superior argument of the death penalty but because he does not know how to respond to the weight of his father's position as a father, as an experienced judge, as a figure he cannot quite grapple with.

Weir of Hermiston centers around the theme of the death penalty. The crucial pages were not completed, but according to Stevenson's stepdaughter Belle, who served as his secretary, Stevenson had planned to have Archie kill a man in a quarrel; he is tried before his own father (a moot point, for in Scottish law a judge was not likely to try his own relatives) and condemned to death. But Archie escapes from prison and, with the young woman he was in love with, flees to America, the judge meanwhile dying of the shock. We cannot say that Stevenson opposed the death penalty any more than Balfour can claim that he favored it in later years, but it was an issue that engaged his most profound thoughts.

Days, months, years grind on at the University. Monotony, boredom. Will Stevenson ever get his degree? He can hardly think of himself as a barrister. Young Stevenson scares some people; others merely think he is showing off. To his velvet jacket and long hair he adds a deep blue shirt, so dark it seems black. A freak. A classmate remembers him as "a queer lank lad with a velvety coat." He is five ten, with a light, resonant voice, fine bones, high cheekbones, brilliant, penetrating eyes that people notice. He knows he makes an impression, but some people do not like him.

Restless and uneasy, he called this unhappy period his "greensickness." He would go for long walks, often stopping on the great bridge that joins Edinburgh's New Town from the old city, and, as he wrote, would "watch the trains smoking out from under, and vanishing into the tunnel on a voyage to brighter skies." Sometimes he would go to the old cemetery, that lay between a prison and a hotel overlooking the railway line. In the shadow of the prison turrets, the sepulchres and the memorials, "In the hot fits of youth, I came to be unhappy." A housemaid in the hotel flirts with him from a window. Once she follows him into the tombs. "Her hair came down, and in the shelter of the tomb my trembling fingers helped her repair the braid." Is he trying to hint at more? He loathes the harsh, wet, middle-class Edinburgh, where people's souls resemble the climate. He yearns to go with the trains to "that Somewhere-else of the imagination where all the troubles are supposed to end." Much of his adult life is to be a search for that place.

Soon his cousin Bob, having studied art in Paris, returns to Edinburgh, helping bring an end to his depression. "The mere return of Bob changed at once and forever the course of my life: I can give you an idea of my relief only by saying that I was at last able to breathe. The miserable isolation in which I had languished was no more in season, and I began to be happy." He adds: "I was done with the sullens for good," a remark that does not take into account at least two major states of near-suicidal depression later on. But for the present, "I had got a good friend I could laugh with." With the abandonment of the wearying, unrewarding study of science, there was a major change in his life. He writes: "I date my departure from three circumstances: natural growth, the coming of friends, and the study of Walt Whitman." He wrote later: "Whitman's *Leaves of Grass*, a book of singular service, a book which tumbled the world upside down for me, blew into space a thousand cobwebs of genteel and ethical illusion, and having thus shaken my tabernacle of lies, set me back again upon a strong foundation of all the original and manly virtues."

In the brief autobiography he dashed off when he was thirty (not all of which has survived) he speaks of his closest friends: Bob, of course; Charles Baxter, who was to remain a close friend throughout Stevenson's life and was to handle many of his legal and business affairs; James Walter Ferrier, an odd, almost hostile young man of great intellect and of "strangeness of a tragic character," who died suddenly a few years later; and Sir Walter Simpson, shy, talented and reserved. The young men enter into a period of collegiate escapades, which at best might be called juvenile. Other biographers give them a chapter or two, but I find them singularly unappealing and prefer to move on to a more interesting passage in Stevenson's life.

✿

A hot, early summer afternoon in 1873. Stevenson, not yet twenty-three, visiting a cousin, Mrs. Churchill Babington, in Suffolk, England, is introduced to a Mrs. Sitwell. A charming scene. Mrs. Fanny Sitwell, Mona Lisa smile, "lush as a houri, but elegant and witty" (so a Margaret Mackay), is stretched out on a sofa in the soft light of a window. An odalisque. Mrs. S.: "I had come to rest and recuperate after a great sorrow and much illness." Mrs. Sitwell—Fanny—is thirty-four, worldly-wise: Ireland, Germany, Australia, India, England are her background. And more, much of which is only hinted at. She was married at seventeen. Husband a clergyman of the Anglo-Irish church, is absent, gone! (A secret drinker, is the rumor.) Mrs. Sitwell must support herself. Little jobs, obtained through friends: translator, reviewer, secretary at a daringly coeducational college in London. Genteel. Two sons, one already dead of a Victorian ailment.

Mrs. Sitwell is something of a myth, a legend in London. A favorite of Henry James, Joseph Conrad. The literary people.

Beautiful.

She smiles. Oh, that smile!

She extends her hand to the young man in the black velvet jacket and straw hat, perspiring in the heat. (He has walked from Bury St. Edmund to Cockfield Rectory, with a heavy knapsack on his back.)

Oh so beautiful!

Stevenson falls in love with her.

He probably has never seen such beauty, such grace . . . such sophistication in raw, grim Edinburgh. Beating heart. Will she?

Mrs. Sitwell, however, is heavily involved, emotionally, with bearded, distinguished Sidney Colvin, age twenty-seven. He is correct, honorable, too honorable for our tastes today. Essayist, critic, already established, someday to be Cambridge Professor of Art, already Slade Professor at the University. But here is young Louis.

Mrs. Babington has earlier said to Mrs. Sitwell: "I do hope you won't mind. He is a very clever, nice fellow, and I think you will like him." Like him? What game is Mrs. Sitwell now playing? "Then the

In wig and gown, Stevenson posed for a formal portrait after receiving his degree from the Scottish bar.

hours began to fly by as they never had flown in that dear, quiet old rectory . . . his talk was like nothing I had ever heard before, though I knew some of our best talkers and writers." She cannot wait to write friend Sidney about friend Louis. Colvin and Stevenson meet in July, immediately become close friends. They have much in common: literature, the arts and Mrs. Sitwell.

Separated by the breadth of England and Scotland from his love object, Stevenson writes her virtually every day in a kind of running journal, saving up the pages until he has a fat packet to mail. "For nearly three years after this [their meeting] Louis wrote me long letters almost daily, pouring out in them all the many difficulties of that time of his life." He takes Mrs. Sitwell to the British Museum. Here he buys a photograph of the Elgin marbles, the Greek statue of the Three Fates stolen by an English adventurer from the greatest of all Hellenic sanctuaries, the Parthenon. The bodies of the headless figures are full, classical, *womanly.* He employs them as a shield in pouring out his desires to Mrs. Sitwell. "They are wonderfully womanly . . . quiet, great-kneed, deep-breasted." "I can think of these three deep-breasted women, living out all their days on remote hilltops, seeing the white dawn and the purple even, and the world outspread before them for ever. . . . If one could love a woman like that once, see her grow pale with passion, and once wring your lips upon hers, would it not be a small thing to die?"

But he has a living woman in mind: "Not that there is not a passion of quite other sort, much less epic, far more dramatic and intimate, that comes out of the very frailty of perishable women; out of the lines of suffering that we see written about their eyes, and that we may wipe out if it were but for a moment; out of the thin hands, wrought and tempered in agony to a fineness of perception that the indifferent or the merely happy cannot know; out of the tragedy that lies about such a love, and the pathetic incompleteness. This is another thing, and perhaps it is a higher."

What Mrs. Sitwell wrote in answer to Stevenson's letters is not known. How did she respond to the current of passion that was directed toward her? She insisted that Stevenson burn her letters to him. Not all of his letters to Mrs. Sitwell (or to anyone else, for that matter) have been published, for, irony, it was Sidney Colvin who edited the first collection of Stevenson's letters.

Though he had been studying for the Bar in Scotland, Stevenson decides that he will enter the English Bar. So in October, 1873, the year he met Mrs. Sitwell, Stevenson goes to London to see about entering the Courts of the Inn and taking the preliminary examination that will enable him to study law there. This will allow him to see Mrs. Sitwell on a regular basis. But Stevenson is physically exhausted and is suffering from a threat of phthisis. His London doctor orders a winter of rest in complete freedom from anxiety and worry. The Riviera is suggested. In November Stevenson returns to Mentone, the resort that he had first visited as a child.

Here he rests in the sun and reads George Sand. His new friend Colvin soon joins him. The two men sit at the same café table day after day writing letters to Mrs. Sitwell. But Stevenson is really low in spirits. He writes Mrs. Sitwell that "Being sent to the South is not much good unless you take your soul with you, you see; and my soul is rarely with me here. . . . If you knew how old I felt! I am sure this is what age brings with it—this carelessness, this disenchantment, this continual bodily weariness. I am a man of seventy: O Medea, kill me, or make me young again!"

But this crush on Mrs. Sitwell may not have been too all-encompassing. At Mentone Stevenson meets two thirtyish Russian aristocratic sisters. The younger one, Mme. Garschine, is "graceful and refined" and Stevenson describes her as "only good-looking after you get to know her a bit." But she flusters him by making very personal remarks and snuggling up to him on the sofa. In the spring of 1874 Stevenson returns to Edinburgh, stopping off at Paris to see Bob Stevenson. Trips to London come whenever he can make them. He is at home never more than two or three months at a time. His relationship with his father improves. His allowance is increased to seven pounds a month. He visits Paris, and a painters' resort near Fontainebleau.

Another great friendship is struck up. The circumstances are different. Leslie Stephen, a prominent editor visiting Edinburgh, meets Stevenson. Stephen takes his young acquaintance to meet another young poet and critic come from London for an operation under the hands of the great Scotch surgeon Lister. Stevenson described the meeting as follows: "Yesterday [13th February, 1875] Leslie Stephen, who was down here to lecture, called on me and took me up to see a poor fellow, a poet who writes for him, and who has been eighteen months in our infirmary, and may be, for all I know, eighteen months more. It was very sad to see him in a little room with two beds, and a couple of children in the other bed; a girl came to visit the children, and played dominoes on the counterpane with them; the gas flared and crackled, the fire burned in a dull, economical way; Stephen and I sat on a couple of chairs, and the poor fellow sat up in his bed with his hair and beard all tangled, and talked as cheerfully as if he had been in a king's palace, or the great King's palace of the blue air."

"Here was no ordinary patient," as Graham Balfour remarks. The poet was William Ernest Henley, lame in one foot from tuberculosis of the bone, the other lost in an amputation. Henley is brilliant, hard drinking, loud talking, gossipy, lovable and hateful, quarrelsome. A poor boy who never was smooth enough for the literary salons he soon entered. He and Stevenson become closest of friends. Stevenson brings him books, including Balzac; his own friends, among them Baxter; a chair, which he carries across town on his head. "In return, he found a friendship based on common tastes in literature and music, the talk of a true poet, the insight of one of the freshest and clearest and strongest of critics, whose training had been free from academic limitations, and whose influence was different in kind from the criticism on which the younger man had learned to rely, though not less full of stimulation and force." Thus Graham Balfour.

Eventually Mrs. Sitwell rebuffs young Stevenson, ever so gently, trying not to damage his sensibilities, for she and Colvin are profoundly locked into one of those delicate Victorian situations which (it is reliably rumored) remain just short of physical consummation—

Stevenson's great friend during his university days and for years after-wards was William Ernest Henley, a rough, hard-drinking poet and editor.

unbearable tension!—since there are the proprieties to consider. Mrs. Sitwell does not dare seek a divorce, nor, presumably, does Colvin press too hard for one, both being aware of the scandal of a clergy-man's wife marrying another man. They will be in their sixties before they feel free to marry. Stevenson, later to enter a similar situation, will act differently. Meanwhile, delicately let down by the woman he craves for, yearns for, Stevenson plunges into a deep depression, close, it seems, to suicide.

But between his writings and his trips to London, his passions with Mrs. Sitwell, his wild oats, Stevenson completes his law studies. On 14 July, 1875, he passes his final examination in the Scottish Bar. He is now entitled to wear a wig and a gown and affix a brass plate bearing his name to the door of the family home at 17 Heriot Row, Edinburgh. From his parents, a gift of a thousand pounds for having passed advocate, and a raise in his allowance to twelve pounds a month. The gift soon disappears, much of it in loans to friends. He is ambiguous about the twelve-pound allowance: sometimes he doesn't cash the checks, other times, when he is in serious financial trouble, his father, through pique or anger, withholds them.

He follows the custom of a daily visit to Parliament House to wait for a case, but clients in need of his particular talents are rare. Result: four known cases, with a total income of a few pounds. He can always argue that he is earning more as a writer, for pieces under the initials R.L.S. appear regularly in *Macmillans, Cornhill* and *Portfolio,* all more or less leading magazines of the time, bringing him some fifty pounds a year. Thus the climax of nine years of University education. Without clients seeking redress of justice, the idler spends more and more time on the top floor of his parents' house, in a little study he has usurped. He also begins to wander, here and there, sometimes alone, more often, on his major expeditions, with Sir Walter Simpson. In 1874 they had made a one-month boat trip off the Scottish coast. "My health is a miracle; I expose myself to rain, and walk, and row, and over-eat myself. I eat. I drink. I bathe in the briny. I sleep," he wrote.

People were beginning to notice him. He would attract one person, repel another. But those who liked him, liked him without reserve. Edmund William Gosse, then a young writer and literary critic and soon to be a pillar of English intellectual life, gives a brief description of Stevenson at the time, when his restlessness was beginning to take a physical shape. "My experience of Stevenson during these first years was confined to London upon which he would make sudden piratical descents, staying a few days or weeks and melting into thin air again. He was much at my house, and it must be told that my wife and I, as young married people, had possessed ourselves of a house too large for our slender means immediately to furnish. The one person who thoroughly approved of our great bare absurd drawing room was Louis, who very earnestly dealt with us on the immorality of chairs and tables, and desired us to sit always, as he delighted to sit, upon hassocks on the floor. Nevertheless, as armchairs and settees straggled into existence, he handsomely consented to use them, although never in the usual way, but with his legs thrown sidewise over the arms of them, or the head of a sofa treated as a perch. In particular, a certain shelf with cupboards below, attached to a bookcase, is worn with the person of Stevenson, who would spend half an evening, while pasionately discussing some question . . . leaping sidewise in a seated posture to the length of this shelf and back again."

Gosse wrote that Stevenson's usual daily routine was to spend the morning working or at business; he would then come to the Saville Club for luncheon, and if he found a congenial friend there, would spend the afternoon in the smoking room "in the highest of spirits and the most brilliant and audacious talk."

"He was simply bubbling with quips and jests. I am anxious that his laughter-loving mood should not be forgotten, because later on it was partly, but I think never wholly quenched, by ill health, responsibility and advance of years.

"His private thoughts and prospects must often have been of the gloomiest, but he seems to have borne his unhappiness with a courage as high as he ever afterwards displayed."

Another friend, Sidney Colvin, on Stevenson: "He had only to speak in order to be recognized in the first minutes for a witty and charming gentleman, and within the first five minutes for a master spirit and man of genius."

And on his absences, many of them sudden and unannounced, Stevenson wrote to his mother, who had complained: "You must not be vexed at my absences, you must understand that I shall be a nomad, more or less, until my days be done. You don't know how I used to long for it in the old days; how I used to go and look at the trains leaving, and wish to go with them. And now, you know, that I have a little more solid under my feet, you must take my nomadic habit as part of me. Just wait until I am in swing and you will see that I shall pass more of my life with you than elsewhere; only take me as I am and give me time. I *must* be a bit of a vagabond."

He bounces back and forth, between Edinburgh, London, the Continent. On one walking trip with Simpson, Stevenson is arrested as a spy by French police. He is alone for a moment, looks suspicious in his odd clothes, and moreover has page after page of undecipherable writings in his knapsack. Simpson, impeccably dressed even on the road, soon appears and rescues Stevenson, for Simpson is *Sir* Walter and his bearing shows it. In Paris, where his cousin Bob has a studio, Stevenson meets a young American artist named Will H. Low. Bob and Low have found an attractive summer resort at a place called Grèz-sur-Loing. A capital place, it is, and Simpson and Stevenson decide they will visit it on their coming canoe trip through the Low Countries and northern France, traveling by rivers and canals. A Great Encounter awaits Stevenson at Grèz.

THE VANDERGRIFTER

NOW we must turn to Mrs. Fanny Van der Grift Osbourne and her family. Mrs. Osbourne—whom everyone calls Fanny, while her future husband is invariably Stevenson—was at the time the wife of one Samuel Osbourne, footloose Kentuckian of great charm and weak morals. His daughter Belle wrote of him: "He was six feet tall, with a good figure, always dressed well, and had a gay likable way with him that made friends everywhere. 'Genial' is not quite the way to describe him. . . . In the prevailing fashion he had a neat golden Van Dyke beard. He was cheerful and laughed often, showing very white teeth." Osbourne's son Lloyd: "He was a tall, very fine-looking man, with a pointed golden beard, and a most winning and lovable nature; I loved him dearly, and was proud of his universal popularity. But he had two eccentricities of which I was much ashamed—he took a cold tub every morning, and invariably slept in pajamas."

Fanny was the daughter of a well-off Indianapolis businessman, Jacob Vandergrift, who had come from Philadelphia, running away from a cruel stepfather. He was in lumber and real estate, sometimes worked for the railroad and had a small farm that was cared for by a hired hand. Fanny's mother, Esther Keens, had also come from Philadelphia; she met Jacob Vandergrift while visiting a sister in Indianapolis. Vandergrift was a great athlete, a good horseman, quick-tempered but lenient with his children. It was the age of spare the rod and spoil the child, but, he believed, "It was best not to interfere with the development of children's characters, but to allow them to have their own way." A recurring rumor in the family (and later among friends and the public) was that Esther Keens had once been secretly married to a Creole and had just as secretly divorced him; Fanny was the child of this mysterious union. This was in apparent explanation of a mystery in the family, for Fanny, in the nineteenth-century phrase, had a touch of the tarbrush about her. Fanny is small, dark, fine-boned, energetic, but above all, "dark." Curly-haired. "Swarthy gypsy beauty," is one description repeated a number of times. Her grand-mother tried to scrub the color out with strong soap and sewed the child's sunbonnet closed to keep her skin from further darkening. A subtle racism runs rampant even in the later biographies: we read references to her "being clever with her little brown hands," "her colour like old ivory," "her unfashionable colouring." Her daughter-in-law, Katharine Durham Osbourne, a woman who hated Fanny for unfathomable reasons, wrote "she belonged to the childhood of the race—the first beginning of civilization—in some dark-skinned peoples."

Fanny's birth is listed as 10 March, 1840, but thanks to the mysterious Creole, she may be three years older than she and the family claim. She is the oldest of five surviving girls and one boy ("all were strong-minded except the boy," writes someone). Fanny, aged two—or five—is baptized in 1842 into the Second Presbyterian Church of Indianapolis by the Reverend Henry Ward Beecher, a noted minister. Like Stevenson she receives a heavy larding of Calvinistic teachings.

Fanny Van der Grift Osbourne, in her mid-thirties, looking much younger than her age.

Grandma brought with her the kind of Presbyterian orthodoxy that embittered Stevenson. "Her religion was of the most terrible kind— the old-fashioned Presbyterianism, which taught that hell was paved with infants' souls, and such horrors," wrote Fanny. But Fanny's mother surprised her with a different view: "I was shocked to hear my mother say she preferred having her children little living devils rather than dead angels."

So Fanny grows up, "an ugly child," on the prairie, riding horses, going her own way, reading early, hating school except for composition, drawing and painting, working in the pioneer crafts, sewing, cooking, making maple sugar, rag rugs, soap and herbal remedies, trying to write a novel. A child of the middle border. Playing with the boys.

The ugly child has a wide circle of admirers. One day, while Fanny, age sixteen, is clumping about the yard on stilts, a young man, Lieutenant Samuel Osbourne, a member of the governor's staff, comes to call. Later: "I'm going to marry Lieutenant Osbourne," announces Fanny to her family. Soon the Lieutenant, too, knows of the decision.

Sam Osbourne, who was said to be a descendant of Daniel Boone, and Fanny Van der Grift, who claimed to be a collateral descendant of Captain James Cook, the great explorer of the Pacific, were married on 4 December, 1857, in their own little red-brick, maple-shaded doll house. Sam was going on twenty and Fanny was seventeen (or twenty). Sam wore a blue coat with brass buttons, a flowered brocade waistcoat and a high lavender stock and fawn trousers. The bride was dressed in a long gown of white satin; her black curls were looped above her ears. "They looked just like children" was the comment.

It is rumored that Fanny is "passionate," hot-blooded; Sam "ardent," romantic. A honeymoon child, Isobel, more commonly called Belle, is born nine months later. Relatives find Fanny cold and distant,

*Fanny Osbourne's rose-covered cottage
in Oakland, with Fanny on the verandah.*

but her younger sister, Nellie, said it was merely a cover for a "real and childlike shyness." It was "the stillness of a frightened wild creature that has never been tamed."

The Civil War breaks out. Sam joins an Indiana regiment and is commissioned a captain. But after six months he resigns to become a member of the Indiana Legion, a kind of militia outfit. Sam can't stick to anything, is the general opinion. In 1862 Sam sells Fanny's share of the family farm to her brother Jacob for $4,000. Fanny never saw the money again. At the end of the next year Sam gives up even the Legion. He abandons Fanny and little Belle, setting off for California with his brother-in-law, George Marshall, husband of Josephine Vandergrift. Stopping in Nevada, Sam prospects for silver.

Eventually Sam sends for Fanny and Belle. They make the difficult trip via the Isthmus of Panama to a primitive site on Nevada's Reese River. It is hard living, in this rough mining town with rough people, rough conditions. Fanny learns to roll her own cigarettes, to use a six-shooter, to handle drunks and lechers. Cool. A remarkable woman. She cooks for some of the miners, among them a nice young English lad named John Lloyd. In the rough camp Lloyd finds the Osbourne shack an oasis. Sam's mine flounders, and the family moves on to Virginia City. Sam picks up a two-bit job as a court reporter. Fanny wonders what Sam does when he is not at work and not at home. Genial Sam. Suddenly Sam takes off for Montana with a friend, also named Sam, to seek out new prospecting sites. Not a word from Sam. Mails are slow, but eventually the suspicion comes to Fanny that Sam is dead. She moves to San Francisco to a "modest" hotel, living on a tiny bit of money saved from the past. Tragedy looms: Word comes that the two Sams, Sam Osbourne and friend, have been killed by Indians in an attack on a mining settlement. Fanny dresses as a widow; black becomes her dark skin. She moves to a cheaper boarding house with Belle, passes herself off as French and becomes a dress-

maker, there being a notion among the Anglo-Saxons that the French
are swarthy. Fanny knows not a word of the French language, but at
least she can support herself and the baby.

She meets John Lloyd again, the young miner from Reese River,
and a friend of his, Timothy Reardon, an up-and-coming lawyer.
Lloyd is now working as a bank clerk; someday he will be president of
the bank, and someday Reardon will be a noted judge. Meanwhile, she
has "safe" little romances with both, particularly with Reardon, writing notes, inviting them to tea, meeting accidentally in the library.

One day the doorbell rings: A big gaunt man is there. He picks up
Belle in his arms, swings her around. It is Sam. He and the other Sam
had strayed away from the rest of the mining party, had escaped the
Indian massacre. Sam is back: charming, restless, shiftless. But charming.

*

The Osbournes resume married life, Sam again working as a court
reporter. Ten dollars a day, big money. He speculates in mining stocks
as a sideline. A son, Samuel Lloyd (named after John Lloyd) is born
in April, 1868. Fanny learns that Sam's sidelines also include one, two,
more young ladies. Quarrels. In July Fanny takes the children and
goes back East to the family farm.

But . . . charming Sam. He has his points, and Fanny is lonely in
Indianapolis. A year later reconciliation comes, followed by Sam buying a new little cottage in East Oakland, in an area known as Brook-
lyn, across the bay from San Francisco. The house stands on the
corner of Eleventh Avenue and East 18th Street. Garden, a verandah,
vines, rose bushes, tiger lilies ("her own particular flower"), a picket
fence. A dream house. A maid to do the chores. Fanny has a studio for
painting in, a darkroom, a rifle range. Her sister Nellie joins them. The
circle of friends grows, friends who are mostly Fanny's: John Lloyd,

Little Belle was distressingly dark, but her mother made the best of her unusual beauty.

Timothy Reardon, some artists, actors, a musician. The intellectual world. Victorian evenings: family musicales, Sam playing the flute, theatricals in the barn, recitations, little parties for the friends. In short, a seemingly happy family. One flaw: Belle's skin. Belle: "I was very dark and of course ashamed of it, but she [her mother] told me it was very nice to be different from other people, and dressed me in crisp yellow linen or pale blue, which made me look still darker. . . . My mother told me to consider my dark skin a beauty, for she believed that if children had a good opinion of themselves they would never be self-conscious." But a striking child!

The year 1871. Sister Nellie: "In the little rose-covered cottage in Oakland a second son, Hervey, was born to the Osbournes. He was an extraordinarily beautiful child, with the rare combination of large dark eyes and yellow curls, but there was an ethereal look about him that boded no long stay on this earthly sphere."

The children remember Sam Osbourne for his charm, suavity, his looks, but these attributes are now causing a void for Fanny. She begins to study art seriously, wins a silver medal for a drawing of the Venus de Milo. Under the surface of happy family, tension builds.

Belle is now in high school, gets attention from a promising (charming) young artist named Joe Strong. Belle, too, takes up Art. It is spelled with a capital A for both daughter and mother.

Fanny feels that life with Sam is a series of strange humiliations. The tension becomes noticeable. Belle writes much later: "They were not happy together, my father and mother. When he was away (he often went off on business trips) home was a pleasant place. . . . When I was alone with my father he was always gay and companionable, but when my mother joined us there was often a tension, an atmosphere of suppressed feelings that chilled me."

Is divorce from the charming, monstrous man possible in this middle-class world? Fanny decides no, even though she has ample grounds. Her alternate escape is to go to Europe to study Art in the midst of Artists. It is now 1875. She and the children and a friend pack up and go off to the Continent. Fanny is thirty-five but looks twenty-five. Sam has agreed to send her a small allowance. It sounds as if, for his part, he is buying some freedom, for Sam's mother once remarked about her son, "Fanny's temper drove him to most of what he did." Nellie: "When she left California for this journey, it is no exaggeration to say that every bond of affection that held her to Samuel Osbourne had been broken."

AN INLAND VOYAGE

AT first they go to Antwerp, where amid the charming cafés, dog-drawn milk carts, women in white-winged caps and the peasants and workers, the ancient streets and squares, the family feels safely comfortable. Fanny tries to write for a living, but while in Europe is able to sell only one article, to the once great *Saint Nicholas*, a magazine for children. She is refused entry to art school in Antwerp because women were not (then) accepted. Little Hervey becomes ill, and the doctor suggests that she take him to Paris for treatment. Paris is also suggested as a place where women could study art. So it is Paris.

❋

An apartment in the fabulous Montmartre, near the Sacré Coeur. Lloyd is entered in a French school, wears a typical school uniform and beret but is called "the Prussian" because he is blond and looks German. Letters come to Fanny saying that Sam Osbourne has been

45

misbehaving and has a "companion" in the rose-covered cottage by the bay. Fanny is both "shocked and deeply grieved."

Hervey falls ill again, wastes away with scrofulous tuberculosis. Later Lloyd wrote: "For weeks he lay dying, while my mother pawned her trinkets to buy him delicacies and toys." He adds graphic touches of Hervey's "wasted baby hands, the burning eyes, the untouched hothouse grapes lying on the counterpane." Fanny could barely meet her bills. "We were miserably poor," Lloyd adds. "It seems to me that I was always hungry. I can remember yet how I used to glue myself to the bakers' windows." The doctors gave up hope for Hervey, but Fanny held on. Hervey called for his father, and Fanny sent for Sam. Osbourne made the long trip, by rail and steamship, arriving in Paris as his son was dying. Hervey's wasted body stopped breathing a few hours later. It was five in the morning. He was given the simple funeral of the French poor. Wrote Lloyd: "We followed him to Père Lachaise where we could only afford one of those temporary French graves, surely the cruelest in the world, from which the bones are flung into the catacombs at the expiration of five years."

Belle remembered that her mother "grew paler and paler, seldom spoke, and it was like being with a ghost." She had fainting spells and lapses of memory. At the atelier where she took art, her sorrowful appearance and sunken eyes made her a good model for tragic subjects.

Lloyd, half-starved, also showed signs of the strain. The doctor advised Fanny to take him away for a rest. An American friend at the atelier suggested an out-of-the-way village named Grèz where poor artists and their mistresses and models went in the summer, some sixty miles from Paris. It was said to be quite respectable and frequented largely by Americans and British. It was a picturesque place, which many artists painted: a low bridge in the center of town, its many arches choked with sedge; rolling green fields; innumerable poplars

Grèz at the time the Stevensons and other foreign artists had discovered it as a summer resort.

and willows; a Norman church; cobbled streets; stone houses; peasants in smocks and archaic dress. So, in April, Sam and Fanny, with Belle and Lloyd, arrived at the Hotel Chevillon, a simple French country inn, whose owners seemed to enjoy a clientele of artists in preference to the usual French bourgeoisie. When the Osbournes arrived the inn was empty but for one artist, another American, but it soon filled up, and they slowly began to forget their sorrow over Hervey. Sam soon found himself bored and restless; this was not the kind of environment he enjoyed, and obviously Fanny, dressed in mourning and still cutting a tragic figure, was not extending herself to make him feel comfortable. The fighting began again, inevitably. Sam now appeared rustic and provincial in his western dress; his charm had little effect on the more sophisticated artists. And Fanny to him seemed affected and snobbish. He soon left for California, his absence being in effect a gift to Fanny.

And now comes a major turning point in Fanny's life: a Stevenson comes to Grèz. The Stevenson is Bob, in a velvet jacket and mustachios, "a dark, roughly dressed man as lithe and as graceful as a Mexican vaquero." Belle's little heart flutters when she sees this romantic artist, something of a poseur but an artist, a man of the world. And then another Stevenson arrives, Bob's cousin Louis. Lloyd's description is as good as any:

"Louis, it seemed, was everybody's hero; Louis was the most wonderful and inspiring of men; his wit, his sayings, his whole piquant attitude towards life were unending subjects of conversation. Everybody said: "Wait till Louis gets here," with an eager and expectant air.

"All my previous fear of him had disappeared, and in its place was a sort of worshipping awe. He had become my hero, too, this wonderful Louis Stevenson, who was so picturesquely gliding towards Grèz in a little sailing canoe, and who camped out every night in a tent.

"Then in the dusk of a summer's day, as we all sat at dinner about the long table d'hôte, some sixteen or eighteen people, of whom my mother and sister were the only women and I the only child, there was a startling sound at one of the open windows giving on the street, and in vaulted a young man with a dusty knapsack on his back. The whole company rose in an uproar of delight, mobbing the newcomer with outstretched hands and cries of greeting. He was borne to a chair; was made to sit down in state, and, still laughing and talking in the general hubbub, was introduced to my mother and sister.

" 'My cousin, Mr. Stevenson,' said Bob, and there ensued a grave

inclination of heads, while I wriggled on my chair, very much overcome, and shyly stole peeps at the stranger. He was tall, straight, and
well-formed, with a fine ruddy complexion, clustering light-brown
hair, a small tawny mustache, and extraordinarily brilliant eyes. But
these details convey nothing of the peculiar sense of power that
seemed to radiate from him—of a peculiar intensity of character that
while not exactly dominating had in its quality something infinitely
more subtle and winning; and he was besides so gay, so sparkling, so
easily the master in all exchange of talk and raillery that I gazed at
him in spell-bound admiration.

"How incredible it would have seemed to me then had some
prophetic voice told me this stranger's life and mine were to run together for nineteen years to come; that I was destined to become his
stepson, his comrade, the sharer of all his wanderings; that we were to
write books together; that we were to sail far-off seas; that we were to
hew a home out of the tropic wilderness; and that at the end, while
the whole world mourned, I was to lay his body at rest on a mountain
peak in Oceania."

✿

Here we see an interesting tableau: an older woman suddenly freed of
her husband, her teenage daughter with the freedom of the American
among a coterie of artists. Two young Scotsmen named Stevenson, one
unbearably dashing, the other so much in the shadow of his older
cousin that he is dismissed as "the other Stevenson." How do the
allegiances line up, considering what we know of the future? Who is
attracted to whom, if at all? We will face the situation in a moment.

Fanny and Belle work hard at painting; they join the artists'
picnics, go bathing in the river (swathed in the usual unwieldy nineteenth-century costumes), go canoeing and rowing, engage in intellectual conversations ("electric and inspiring," so Belle wrote). But it

was Bob who stands out for Fanny, for he is "exactly like one of Ouida's heroes," referring to a current romantic author, "with the hand of steel in the glove of velvet." Fanny thinks that Bob is "the best painter here, a charming musician, speaks all languages, does all sorts of feats of strength and has no ambition." Hardly a word in her letters about "the other Stevenson."

But Belle sees the pair indifferently. Of the other Stevenson she writes, "There is a young Scotsman here, a Mr. Stevenson, who looks at me as though I were a natural curiosity. He never saw a real American girl before, and he says I act and talk as though I came out of a book—I mean an American book. . . . He is such a nice looking ugly man, and I would rather listen to him talk than read the most interesting book I ever saw. We sit in the little green arbor after dinner drinking coffee and talking late at night. Mama is ever so much better and getting prettier every day." Stevenson finds Belle such a prime example of an American type of young woman that he writes a magazine article about her. He goes off briefly to Britain and then, with his friend, young Sir Walter Simpson, takes a canoe trip from Antwerp along the Scheldt and Belgian canals, eventually landing at Grèz. Out of it he gets his first short book, *An Inland Voyage.*

Is there a shifting of interests? Bob takes Fanny for a walk. They get lost in the forest, an incident Fanny mentions in one of her regular letters to Reardon back in San Francisco. Irritation on Reardon's part. Fanny must explain:

"You spoke of my getting lost—for the purposes of flirtation. I would hardly do that with one considered a madman, though his conversation seemed to my limited understanding quite logical and sensible. I think if you heard it all you would hardly call it flirtation, though. Of course, I know less about such things than a man of your varied experience. This is what he was saying to me; that I was a stunning, good little girl, not a 'toothless old hag,' though that was a

The American artist Will Low painted a portrait of Stevenson and an un-identified companion sprawled beneath a tree at Grèz. This was in 1875, the year before Fanny Osbourne arrived.

politeness I dare say. And that he wanted to tell me something . . . that I would make no mistake in cultivating the acquaintance of his, Mr. Stevenson's cousin, Louis. 'You must have nothing to say to *me*,' he said, 'for I am only a vulgar cad, but Louis is a gentleman, and you can trust him and depend on him.' And he thanked me for not laughing at Louis, whose faintings and hysterics were caused by ill health. And then . . . we found we had taken the wrong path home," Fanny continues to the poor Reardon, who apparently had a conflict between his proper views and his romantic curiosity about Fanny. "I took his advice because it was honestly given and kindly meant, and I think I should like him better than some of the other men, except that he reminds me in some curious ways of you. He was right about his cousin, whom I like very much and who is the wittiest man I ever met. Only I do wish he wouldn't burst into tears in such an unexpected way; it is so embarrassing. One doesn't know what to do, whether to offer him a pocket hankerchief [as she spells it], or look out of the window."

Was Bob trying to get Fanny out of the way because he was attracted to Belle, who had a crush on one Frank O'Meara, an Irishman described by Will Low, one of the Americans at Gréz, as "an artist of peculiary delicacy and charm"? Or had Stevenson spoken to him about directing Fanny in his direction? There is a shifting of alliances, of interests.

Lloyd notices.

"Young as I was I could not help noticing that R L S and my mother were greatly attracted to each other; or rather how they would sit and talk interminably on either side of the dining-room stove while everybody else was out and busy. I grew to associate them as always together, and in a queer, childish way I think it made me very happy. I had grown to love Luly Stevenson, as I called him; he used to read the *Pilgrim's Progress* and the *Tales of a Grandfather* to me, and tell me stories 'out of his head'; he gave me a sense of protection and warmth, and though I was far too shy ever to have said it aloud, he seemed so much like *Greatheart* in the book that this was my secret name for him.

"When autumn merged into early winter and it was time for us to return to Paris, I was overjoyed when my mother said to me: 'Luly is coming, too.' "

The Osbournes move into a building in Montmartre inhabited by some other foreigners, including Americans. Stevenson, living not far away, visits Fanny daily along with Bob and Will Low. Knowing that his family is not going to take favorably to Fanny, Stevenson writes them elliptically about a party at the studio of an art student: "One of the matrons was a very beautiful woman indeed; I played old fogy and had a deal of talk with her which pleased me."

In October Stevenson picks up an eye infection so serious he nearly loses his sight. Fanny insists that he stay at her apartment so she can nurse him better. Discretion is ignored. She wires Bob for help, but he is ill, and then she appeals to Sidney Colvin. She brings Stevenson to London for treatment. She herself must undergo surgery on her foot, which she had injured in a boating accident at Grèz. The winter goes on, with Fanny and Belle at work in the atelier, parties and dinners out on slim budgets. Stevenson keeps on writing—slight, inconsequential pieces, getting published here and there. An editor gives a favorable review of his work, referring to him as "one Stevenson." And then another summer at Grèz, this time there being no doubt that Louis Stevenson and not Bob is Fanny's constant companion. His friends have met Fanny. They do not take to her, and are coldly objective in their appraisals. The pros and cons seem to break down along national lines.

Another American, Birge Harrison, recalls that she was "a grave and remarkable type of womanhood, with eyes of a depth and somber beauty that I have never seen equaled—eyes nevertheless that upon occasion could sparkle with humor and brim over with laughter. Yet on the whole Mrs. Osbourne impressed me as first of all a woman of profound character and serious judgment, who could, if occasion called, have been the leader in some great movement. But she belonged to the quattrocentro [fourteenth] rather than the nineteenth century. Had she been born a Medici, she would have held rank as one of the most remarkable women of all time." He adds: "Mrs. Osbourne was in no sense ordinary. Indeed, she was gifted with a mysterious sort of overintelligence, which is almost impossible to describe, but

A watercolor of a French peasant by Stevenson done at Grèz.

which impressed itself upon everyone who came within the radius of her influence. Napoleon had much of this; likewise his arch-enemy, the great Duke of Wellington; and among women, Catherine of Russia and perhaps Elizabeth of England. She was, therefor, both physically and mentally, the very antithesis of the gay, hilarious, open-hearted

Stevenson, and for that reason perhaps the woman in all the world best fitted to be his life comrade and helpmate."

Colvin saw her in Napoleonic terms also: "Her personality was almost as vivid as Stevenson's. She was small, dark-complexioned, eager, devoted; of squarish build—supple and elastic; her hands and feet were small and beautifully modelled, though busy; her head had a crop of close-waving thick black hair. She had a build and character that somehow suggested Napoleon, with a firm setting of jaw and beautifully precise and delicate modelling of the nose and lips; her eyes were full of sex and mystery as they changed from fire or fun to gloom or tenderness." Colvin also remarked about her "fine pearly set of small teeth, and the clear metallic accents of her intensely human and often quaintly individual speech."

THE AMATEUR EMIGRANT

BY now—1878—Stevenson's and Fanny's attachment is openly observed and acknowledged. Stevenson is twenty-eight, Fanny thirty-eight and pushing thirty-nine (or is she forty-one?). Although his allowance has recently been increased to one hundred pounds a year and he still has some of the thousand-pound gift from the time of his degree, he is in serious financial straits. He is faced with the problem of having to support Fanny and her children, for Sam is as unreliable a provider as he was a husband. Stevenson now believes he should put the matter of his relationship with Mrs. Osbourne before his father. In February, not believing he could discuss the situation comfortably in Edinburgh, he takes the unusual step of asking Thomas Stevenson to come to Paris, making the request with the help of both Mrs. Sitwell and Colvin. "Don't be astonished," he writes Colvin about what must have seemed an unprecedented act of daring in straight-laced Victorian age, "but admire my courage and Fanny's. We wish to be right with the world as far as we can. . . . Three days from hence, I shall know where I am, and either be quite well off or quite a beggar."

Thomas Stevenson made the trip. He saw certain difficulties in the situation: Mrs. Osbourne was legally tied to another man who was some six thousand miles away; she was older than Louis, and practically speaking, he suspected the affair would fade away in time. For the present he was prepared to be "decent" to his tubercular son.

In return for his father's visit to Paris, Stevenson goes to Edinburgh for Easter, leaving the Osbournes alone in Paris. Fanny had been ill for quite some time, a vague kind of illness that did not respond to treatment. Stevenson wrote Mrs. Sitwell: "I wish I could say she is well: her nerves are quite gone; one day I find her in heaven and the next in hell. We have many strong reasons for getting her out of Paris in about a month."

Fanny's running problem is whether or not she should return to the States in an effort to find a way out of the impasse she is in. In France she and Stevenson had a kind of acceptable relationship, tolerated among the artists and among the French, who barely knew her. But the proprieties of Victorian England and Scotland prevent the couple from living together there, and they can hardly return to America under the same circumstances. Meanwhile Stevenson continues to write. *An Inland Voyage* appears in May, bringing him twenty pounds and some good reviews. His own—critical—view of it ("not badly written, thin, mildly cheery and strained") is an accurate observation. And Fanny accepts the fact that she is not to be a major artist. Her writing talents are channeled to suggestions to others, a practice Stevenson puts up with, tolerates and sometimes profits by, but which can infuriate other people.

A third summer at Grèz begins for the Osbournes, with Stevenson visiting them from time to time. In July Fanny suddenly decides that she will return to San Francisco with the children. There seems to be a crisis with Sam. He has written that he is tired of sending money and that she must come home; and Stevenson is unable to do more than give token aid, his great plea to his father having come to little.

A terrifying step, this parting of two people who are now beginning their third year together, two people deeply tied to each other, who are now involved in a ruthless decision. What is to happen once they are separated?

The Osbournes go to London, on the way to the boat train for the transatlantic steamer. Stevenson is there, working with Henley on a small magazine. And then . . .

Lloyd Osbourne: "Meanwhile the hour of parting was drawing near. I had not the slightest perception of the quandary my mother and R L S were in, nor what agonies of mind their approaching separation was bringing; and doubtless I prattled endlessly about 'going home,' and enjoyed all our preparations, while to them that imminent August spelled the knell of everything that made life worth living. But when the time came I had my own tragedy of parting, and the picture lives with me as clearly as though it were yesterday. . . . The moment to say goodbye had come. It was a terribly short and sudden and final, and before I could realize it R L S was walking away down the long length of the platform, a diminishing figure in a brown ulster. My eyes followed him, hoping that he would look back. But he never turned, and finally disappeared in the crowd. Words cannot express the sense of bereavement, of desolation that suddenly struck at my heart. I knew I would never see him again."

✺

San Francisco. Sam Osbourne has a good job, court clerk in the Bureau of Mines. Same old rose-covered cottage. Sam seems bland, a bit on the dull side, but warm-hearted. Belle: "He was as gay and entertaining as ever, but at home there was a perceptible chill between him

Stevenson with his donkey Modeste. The picture shows various scenes from the book, with the final vignette of the author and beast disappearing into the sunset.

and my mother." Fanny's sister Nellie is there.

A year passes, in anguish. Scenes behind closed doors with Sam. Fanny barely writes to Stevenson for six months. In the spring Sam and Fanny take off on a "little trip," apparently to make another attempt at healing the rift between them. A week later, from the old Spanish town of Monterey, 150 miles south of San Francisco, they send for the children.

Picturesque town. Narrow, crooked streets, fishing boats, people on horses, old cannons, high adobe walls, orange-tiled roofs, iron grilles, flowers all over. Sam leaves his family here, in the old Spanish home of one Señora Bonifacio, proud old Spanish lady living in reduced circumstances and forced to take in boarders. Sam returns to the rose-covered cottage with his latest friend. Belle again: "It shocks me now to remember how little I noticed that my father's visits grew fewer and fewer. At first he joined us over the weekends, going back to San Francisco on Sunday nights; then several weeks would pass, and often when he did come, Nellie and I would be sent away while he and my mother held agitated conferences. I know now they were discussing a divorce."

But Sam is not all bad. He buys three small Canadian saddle horses for Fanny, Belle and Nellie and a pony for Lloyd. Fanny's health improves in the fine sea air and bright sun.

Belle has a suitor, her old San Francisco friend Joe Strong, the dashing, impecunious young artist originally from Hawaii. More romance. Nellie, too, has a suitor, one Adulfo Sanchez, saloon-keeper whose family, once aristocratic landowners, have lost their money.

Riding parties, picnics, serenades, fiestas, Nellie and Adulfo announcing their engagement. But Belle and Joe must wait, for he is a struggling young portrait painter and commissions are scarce.

A period of marking time begins. Stevenson keeps on writing— essays, short stories, poems. But so few letters to Mrs. Osbourne. "To

F. I never write letters," he told Colvin. "All that people want by letters has been done between us. We are acquainted; why go on with more introductions? I cannot change so much, but that she could still have the clue and recognize every thought." A strange remark. Have they had a falling out? His friends aren't sure what is in his head. He seems seriously distraught. *An Inland Voyage* has some modest sales and acclaim. Stevenson is puzzled that the public finds it better than he does. Later he will take a similar trip, to be written up as *Travels with a Donkey*, in the company of a recalcitrant beast named Modeste; it is an undistinguished, pleasant work ("It has some good passages. I can say no more"). He collaborates with Henley on a play about a Scottish underworld figure named Deacon Brodie, an interest since his teens. In all, he and Henley are to work together on four plays, but only *Deacon Brodie* has any success.

Some small payments come in, but never enough. His father sends Stevenson twenty-five pounds every quarter, but the checks are often uncashed, as Stevenson is trying to be independent. "I must save, save, save," he writes Colvin. "£350 must be made and laid by ere I can breathe freely. I sit and sit, and scribe and scribe, but cannot get my back into it." But even with his own financial problems, he sends twenty-five pounds out of his own account to Fanny's brother Jake in southern California. Presumably the money is actually meant for Fanny. News comes that Fanny is ill. "Brain fever" is the phrase that Stevenson uses. It has been a disquieting spring for Stevenson—it is now 1879. With a grasshopper restlessness he goes from Swanston, where he and Henley are working, to London, back to Swanston, then on a short trip with his parents, to London again, to France for a walking trip, back to London. The young man cannot settle in any one place. He writes to a friend, Gosse, "I want—I want—I want—a holiday; I want to be happy; I want the moon or something. I want the object of my affections badly anyway."

A trip to America is shaping up . . . but. Edmund Gosse: "Louis's family and the inner circle of his friends were equally certain that it was neither needful nor expedient that he should make this journey." Gosse adds that it was hoped that the withdrawal of "supplies"—a euphemism for money—would make the voyage "impossible." Stevenson approaches the editor of the famed *Times* of London, trying to obtain an assignment as a traveling correspondent. The editor offers him a job in London. No, Stevenson wants to do some articles abroad. Specifically in the States. California, that is. While Stevenson was in France with Modeste the donkey, he had written his mother for fifty pounds; because of the state of tension with his father, and the various uncashed checks, he had not been paid in six months. Now he needs the money. No deal with the *Times*. Back to Edinburgh on 14 July. A telegram has come from Fanny. For years, friends, relatives, the public have speculated about the contents: beseeching, angry, loving, beckoning, rejecting, hurt, desperate? A mystery. But whatever, Stevenson must go immediately to California. All hesitations are shaken, a year of indecision is ended.

The Gosses, husband and wife, "to the last were trying to dissuade him from what seemed to us the maddest of enterprises." After an evening of trying to talk Stevenson out of the trip, both Gosse and Stevenson are in a "pretty hysterical state." Henley: "Withal, if he wanted a thing, he went after it with an entire contempt of consequences." Thus, cutting off "supplies" was fruitless.

Friends are convinced the trip will be a disaster. Career will be ruined. Brilliant young writer finished, destroyed in pursuit of aging, faded American fortune hunter!

And his parents! Stevenson did not even tell them that he was going to see Fanny. Mrs. Stevenson had written in her diary that she and her husband had expected Louis to go with them to a health resort, but that "he meets us at the train and tells us that he is called

Stevenson looks eager and fit in this heavily retouched photograph taken as he was about to embark for California, but he was beset by anxieties. He signed the passenger list as "Robert Stephenson."

away on business—this is on the 30th July and we heard later that he has started for America." Stevenson, however, must have been in despair over his handling of the turn of events, for he was not a liar or a sneak. In his farewell note to Colvin he says, "I seemed to have died last night." He then adds, "I can say honestly I have at this moment neither a hope, or fear, or an inclination." In his letter to Colvin, Stevenson encloses a note to his parents. After Colvin forwarded it, Thomas Stevenson wrote him, "For God's sake use your influence. Is it fair that we should be half murdered by his conduct? I am unable to write more about this sinful mad business." The father saw "nothing but destruction to himself as well as to all of us" in his son's sudden departure.

Stevenson has thirty pounds for the trip, all he could scrape together. He has decided to travel as an emigrant. Steerage passage is six guineas, but for the sake of a tiny cabin where he can write he pays another two guineas. He has booked passage on the *Devonia*. He steps aboard ship, having abandoned, as far as he or anyone else knew, everything in his life except his love for a faraway woman who had sent him a mysterious cablegram.

✺

A ten-day voyage on the *Devonia*, uneventful except for some rough weather. Stevenson spends much of his time on a story, "The Story of a Lie," which he posts later to Colvin. He writes thirty-one pages during the voyage. He tells Colvin: "I am not very well; bad food, bad air and hard work have brought me down. But the spirits keep good." He hopes that if the voyage did not at least lead to a series of articles, it would at least form the first part of a new book. "The last weight on me has been trying to keep notes for this purpose. Indeed I have worked like a horse and am tired as a donkey." His fellow passengers were not hardy pioneers, he soon realizes, but failures and alcoholics, seasick and drunk. His notes are excellent. The portraits of the lower depths of a European peasant and industrial world drifting into America form a valuable addition to nineteenth-century history, yet a curious thing happened on the way to publication. This section of Stevenson's *The Amateur Emigrant* was not published until after Stevenson's death; when his father realized the conditions under which his son had traveled, he bought back the publication rights from the publisher. Even the standard editions contained deletions of passages Stevenson's friends thought too raw for the public. The full text was not released until 1966.

Stevenson worries that if he continues to work at such a grueling pace, "I shall have nothing but my fine bones to bring to port." He asks, almost to himself: "What shall I find over here? I dare not wonder." He despises the first-class passengers who come down to slum in steerage. He loses a stone in weight—that is, fourteen pounds. He cannot eat, has constant constipation, has an itch that will not go away.

At last the ship arrives in New York, in a pouring rainstorm. It is a Sunday. With another emigrant, Stevenson finds quarters in Mitchell's Reunion House, near the docks. A French restaurant offers food he can eat. He is to leave by emigrant train on Monday evening for California, and has only the day for "a thousand and one things to do."

"It rained with patient fury; every now and then I had to get under cover for a while in order, so to speak, to give my mackintosh a rest. . . . I went to banks, post-offices, rail-way offices, restaurants, publishers, booksellers, moneychangers, and wherever I went a pool would gather about my feet, and those who were careful would look on with an unfriendly eye." At the General Delivery window of the post office he finds a letter from Fanny; she has "inflammation of the brain," he writes Henley. The rain continues. "The only American institution which has yet won my respect is the rain. One sees it is a new country, they are so free with their water," he writes Colvin as he prepares to board the train. In *The Amateur Emigrant*: "I was so wet when I got back to Mitchell's towards the evening, that I simply had to divest myself of my shoes, socks, and trousers, and leave them behind for the benefit of New York City. No fire could have dried them ere I had to start; and to pack them in their present condition was to spread ruin among my other possessions. With a heavy heart I said farewell to them as they lay in a pulp in the the middle of a pool upon the floor of Mitchell's kitchen." A foolish act for a poor man.

Someone else would have wrapped them separately and tried to salvage them later.

Anyway, off to the train he goes, aided by a porter hired by Mitchell. A crowd of emigrants from a number of ships has assembled at the ferry slip at West Street, and they are taken to the train at Jersey City, where Stevenson settles aboard an emigrant car, his abandoned clothes having been replaced by a set of George Bancroft's *History of the United States* in six volumes.

At last the trip has begun. Stevenson faces twelve days of wearying travel. It is impossible to lie down, and the first day of travel there is no food available, though the scenery is magnificent as they travel through Pennsylvania. He stands on the platform by the hour watching the pleasant, shapely villages flash by, hearing the voices and the animals sounds, seeing the colors of fields and sky, mountains and waterways, smelling the earth and the woods. "I began to exult with myself upon this rise in life like a man who had come into a rich estate." But, the next day, bowling through Ohio, his mood has changed. In a letter to Colvin: "I had no idea how easy it was to commit suicide. There seems nothing left of me; I died a while ago; I do not know who it is that is travelling." But he concludes the letter on a more optimistic note: "No man is any use until he has dared everything; I feel just now as if I had, and so might become a man. . . . I will not say die, and do not fear man nor fortune."

If the ship had been bad, the train was worse. Emigrants were considered barely human, and the facilities for them were sadly inadequate. Food was obtained from pedlars who boarded at various stops. The passengers had only wooden benches upon which to sit and sleep. The passage through the Black Hills of Wyoming, which Stevenson had looked forward to, seemed worse than other parts of the trip: "The sleepers lay in uneasy attitudes; here two chums alongside, flat upon their backs like dead folk; there a man sprawling upon the

This battered photograph of Stevenson and Belle is undated, but it may have been taken in San Francisco in 1879. Later the Samoans thought Belle was Stevenson's daughter by an island woman.

floor, with his face upon his arm; there another half-seated with his head and shoulders on the bench. The most passive were continually and roughly shaken by the movement of the train; others stirred, turned, or stretched out their arms like children; it was surprising how men groaned and murmured in their sleep; and as I passed to and fro, stepping across the prostrate, and caught now a snore, now a gasp, now a half-formed word, it gave me a measure of the worthlessness of rest in that unresting vehicle. Although it was chill, I was obliged to open my window, for the degradation of the air soon became intolerable to one who was awake and using the full supply of life."

And when day comes: "Mile upon mile, and not a tree, a bird, or a river. Only down the long, sterile canons, the train shot hooting, and awoke the resting echo." Most of the time Stevenson sat atop the train with the other people, to escape the heat and the fetid air of the wooden cars. The emigrants are abysmally poor. Stevenson writes Henley: "We have a tin wash-bowl among four. I wear nothing but a shirt and a pair of trousers. . . . It is a strange affair to be an emigrant." Atop the car he can see the track straight before and straight behind to either horizon. "Peace of mind I enjoy with extreme serenity; I am doing right; I know no one will think so; and don't care. . . . I don't eat; but, man, I can sleep." Then he becomes even more ill: "What is it to become ill in an emigrant train let those declare who know. I slept none till late this morning, overcome with laudanum, of which I had luckily a little bottle. All to-day I have eaten nothing, and only drunk two cups of tea, for each of which, on the pretext that the one was breakfast, and the other dinner, I was charged fifty cents."

Sometimes he sits on the tiny platform between cars, watching the scenery, the towns, the people. He makes some observations, which go smack into the conclusion of the published editions of *The Amateur Emigrant*, which are totally ignored: The chapter is called Despised Races. It begins: "Of all stupid ill-feelings, the sentiment of my fellow-Caucasians towards our companions in the Chinese car was the most stupid and the worst. They seemed never to have looked at them, listened to them, or thought of them, but hated them *a priori*. . . . My emigrants declared the Chinese were dirty . . . but their efforts at cleanliness put the rest of us to shame." And he continues in a true appreciation of their civilization: "For my own part I could not look but with wonder and respect on the Chinese. Their forefathers watched the stars before mine had begun to keep pigs. Gunpowder and printing, which the other day we imitated, and a school of manners which we never had the delicacy so much as to desire to imitate, were theirs in a long past antiquity. They walk the earth with us, but it seems they must be of different clay. . . ." And so on, for a long passage of appreciation of what the Chinese have given to the world and what they are. And then he shifts to another race, "the noble red man . . . over whose own hereditary continent we had been steaming all these days." He writes: "The silent stoicism of their conduct, and the pathetic degradation of their appearance, would have touched any thinking creature, but my fellow passengers danced and jested round them with a truly Cockney baseness. I was ashamed for the thing we call civilization. We should carry upon our consciences so much, at least, of our forefathers misconduct as we continue to profit by ourselves."

His concluding paragraph is worth printing in full, for it states the plight of the oppressed concisely and in terms that have not lost their point:

"If oppression drives a wise man mad, what should be raging in the hearts of these poor tribes, who have been driven back, step after step, their promised reservations torn from them one after another as the States extended westward, until at length they are shut up into these hideous mountain deserts of the centre—and even there find themselves invaded, insulted, and hunted out by ruffianly diggers? The eviction of the Cherokees (to name but an instance), the extortion of Indian agents, the outrages of the wicked, the ill-faith of all, nay, down to the ridicule of such poor beings as were here with me upon the train, make up a chapter of injustice and indignity such as a man must be in some ways base if his heart will suffer him to pardon or forget. These old, well-founded, historical hatreds have a saviour of nobility for the independent. That the Jew should not love the Christian, nor the Irishman love the English, nor the Indian brave tolerate the thought of the American, is not disgraceful to the nature of man; rather, indeed, honourable, since it depends on wrongs ancient like the race, and not personal to him who cherishes the indignation."

*

Finally the weary emigrants reach Sacramento; the next morning before dawn they are at the Oakland side of San Francisco Bay. "The day was breaking as we crossed the ferry; the fog was rising over the citied hills of San Francisco; the bay was perfect—not a ripple, scarce a stain, upon its blue expanse, everything was waiting, breathless, for the sun. A spot of cloudy gold lit first upon the head of Tamalpais, and then widened downward on its shapely shoulder; the air seemed to awaken, and began to sparkle, and suddenly . . . the city of San Francisco, and the bay of gold and corn, were lit from end to end with summer daylight."

*

Lloyd Osbourne: "One morning in our sitting room my mother looked down at me rather oddly, and, with a curious brightness in her eyes, said, 'I have news for you. Luly's coming.' "

A scarecrow appears on Señora Bonifacio's doorsill. It is Stevenson, in his worn blue serge suit and bowler hat, fortified by a stiff drink he has just picked up in a local saloon. His wrists are red from his shipboard itch, he looks worn and haggard. Who is this strange man, visiting this strange lady whose husband has lately ignored her? The ladies of Monterey now refer to her as "that Mrs. Osbourne." She has short hair and smokes cigarettes, and her daughter is said to be involved with an impecunious artist. Now a scarecrow stands before her, comes to visit her daily, walks with her on the street. Poverty and ill health are joined to poverty and ill health. Two castaways in sunny Monterey.

Lloyd Osbourne: "I remember his walking into the room, and the outcry of delight that greeted him; the incoherence, the laughter, the tears; the heart-welling joy of reunion. Until that moment I had never thought of him as being in ill health. On the contrary, in vigor and vitality he had always seemed among the foremost of those young men at Grèz. Now he looked ill, even to my childish gaze; the brilliancy of his eyes emphasized the thinness and pallor of his face. His clothes, no longer picturesque but merely shabby, hung loosely on his shrunken body; and there was about him an indescribably lessening of his alertness and self-confidence.

"This fleeting impression passed away as I grew more familiar with him in our new surroundings. Certainly he had never seemed gayer nor more light-hearted, and he radiated laughter and good spirits. His talk was all about the people he was meeting, and he gave me my first understanding of the interest to be derived from human nature."

"My news is nil," Stevenson writes Baxter within a few days. "I know nothing. I go out camping." It seems like the end, for the next few words seem to say that after this bottomless trip through the lower depths, all is over. ". . . And now say good-bye to you, having had the itch and a broken heart."

Had Fanny spurned Stevenson, this ragged man?

He itches, he scratches here and there, trying to keep the scratching unnoticeable, genteel. People of his station do not get the emigrant's itch. Scratch, scratch, scratch, on his pale, tightly drawn skin, like some damned farmhand, slum dweller. Constipated. He has a cough. He is exhausted. Robert Louis Stevenson, end of the line of lighthouse builders, writer of slight books and light pieces, critically

Kidnapped

successful but financially dependent on his angry father, is at the
end.

Mrs. Osbourne, a lady in her own poverty, has not quite spurned
him, but she is undecided. Not too far away in San Francisco is old
friend John Lloyd, a rising banker, stiff, dependable, like one's image
of bankers, willing to aid her in little ways, though he seems thankful
that he has not become entangled in this semidivorcée and her chil-

dren. Has she ever thought that perhaps she might have spent her time more profitably if she had gone after John Lloyd . . . or lawyer of promising future Timothy Reardon?

So, Fanny is undecided. But Stevenson is shaken. He aches inside. For once he is unable to write. He hires a horse and wagon to wander off into the fragrant pine-scented mountains south of Monterey, above the Carmel Valley. After eighteen miles he collapses: "Two nights I lay out under a tree in a sort of stupor, doing nothing but fetch water for myself and horse, light a fire and make coffee." He is found nearly dead by two shepherds. To Colvin: "I was camping out, but got so sick that the two rancheros took me in and tended me. One is an old bear-hunter, seventy-two years old, and a captain from the Mexican war; the other a pilgrim, and one who was out with the bear flag and under Frémont when California was taken by the States. They are both true frontiersmen, and most kind and pleasant. Captain Smith, the bear-hunter, is my physician, and I obey him like an oracle." Stevenson teaches the ranch children reading, works on his notes from the voyage. "I will not deny that I feel lonely to-day; but I do not fear to go on, for I am doing right . . . if you knew all I have been through, you would wonder I had done so much as I have." The burning creative fire has returned. Though death has brushed him, his notes are shaping up into *The Amateur Emigrant*. Death has almost enveloped him, under the fierce light sky, so starry at night, in the sweet-smelling mountains. To Colvin he sends his epitaph, should death really strike him down, the draft of a poem, "Requiem."

> Under the wide and starry sky
> Dig the grave and let me lie . . .

Then to Gosse he writes: "I had a week's misery and a fortnight's illness," a rather cryptic statement for anyone who did not know the details. Then: "There is a wonderful callousness in human nature which enables us to live." So, it was back to Fanny, with a renewed, different, positive point of view. Such tension there must have been in Fanny Osbourne's life that past year, between Sam Osbourne on one side and Robert Louis Stevenson on the other! But one tension was negative, destructive, banal, vitiating, while the other, even with its problems (health and finances) was positive and loving. For when Stevenson came down from the mountains, looking and feeling quite a bit better, Fanny realized that she had almost lost him. It was clear to her that she loved this sickly, destitute, ragged writer, whose promise was all literary and not financial. And it was clear to Stevenson that he had followed the proper course: "In coming here I did the right thing," he wrote to Colvin. "I have not only got Fanny patched up again and in health, but the effect of my arrival has straightened up everything." Fanny decided that she would try to obtain a divorce the following January under private circumstances. Stevenson to Colvin: "Yours truly will be a married man as soon thereafter as the law and decency permit. The only question is whether I shall be alive for the ceremony."

Fanny has been won. A minor skirmish with Belle develops. Belle years later tells a Mrs. Elsie Noble Caldwell (in *Last Witness for R.L.S.*) that she resented Louis's coming to Monterey. Mrs. Caldwell about Belle: "She had not the compassion to realize how much Louis, sick and weak and fighting utter discouragement in the constant rejection of his writing, depended on her mother's cheering society and her hearty midday meal—for him food for the mind and spirit even more than the body." " 'Louis's conduct,' Belle recalled, 'was not that of a romantic lover who had followed a sweetheart halfway around the world. Although he was gay and full of banter, he was almost coldly casual towards my mother—and her attitude not much different toward him, except her constant care in providing his preference in

food, such as hot baking-powder biscuits which he insisted upon calling little cakes.

"'Maybe my mother saw in this contrast to my father the security
from infidelity that had wrecked their marriage. At any rate she was
happy when he was near, and I, standing in awe of her inflexible
decisions, had no hopeful moments that she would not marry this
penniless foreigner. At seventeen I would sit in judgment to be re-
gretted in shame for the rest of my life.'"

So, Belle admits that the situation between Stevenson and her
mother contributes to her own elopement with Joe Strong, bon vivant
and artist, and leading figure of San Francisco Bohemian circles. She
does not know that it is Stevenson who prevents Fanny from rushing
off to San Francisco to stop the marriage.

Later Belle writes: "Though I admired Louis and respected him,
there had always been a hidden antagonism between us. Perhaps because I had adored my father, I was unconsciously critical of him."
However she admits of her mother and Stevenson that "at any rate,
she was happy when he was near."

Money gone, Stevenson works away in an unheated, barely fur-
nished room in the French Hotel, an old adobe building (now pre-
served by the state as The Stevenson House), on *The Amateur
Emigrant*, finishing half of it by October 8, and then turning to other
pieces. Toward the end of the month he sends the entire nine chapters
of *The Pavillion on the Links* to Henley; it is bought by *Cornhill*
magazine. Money is his constant preoccupation, and almost every letter makes some mention of it. To Henley: "May it [*Pavillion*] bring
me money for myself and my sick one, who may need it, I do not know
how soon."

Lloyd, writing later: "I was old enough to appreciate how poor
he was, and it tore at my boyish heart that he should take his meals at
a grubby little restaurant with men in their shirt sleeves, and have so

bare and miserable a room in the old *adobe* house on the hill. Conceive my joy, therefore, when one day he burst in with the news of a splendid job, and prolonged the suspense by making us all try to guess what it was; and my crushing disappointment when it turned out to be as a special reporter on the local paper at two dollars a week.

"It was supposed to be a great joke, and I laughed with the rest; but on my part it was a sad and wondering pretence. Two dollars meant eight meals at the fisherman's restaurant. What was to become of poor Luly, who daily looked thinner and shabbier. But afterward my mother reassured me, and I was thrilled to hear of what 'experience' meant to a writer, and how in reality Monterey was a kind of gold mine in which Luly was prospering extraordinarily, little though he looked it."

The joke of the matter was that the two dollars a week was given to the newspaper by friends of Stevenson's in Monterey who could not stand seeing him continue in his poverty.

But Stevenson and Fanny are not to spend too much time together in Monterey. In the middle of October (1879) she decides she must return to San Francisco with her children to pursue the divorce. Reardon, rather reluctantly, is handling the papers. She takes up residence in the rose-bowered cottage contaminated by Sam's infidelities, leaving Stevenson alone in Monterey, with his chills and his work. He develops pleurisy in the winter fogs. "I am going for thirty now," he writes Gosse, "and unless I can snatch a little rest before long, I have, I may tell you in confidence, no hope of seeing thirty-one." To Baxter: "With my parents all looks black." To Henley: "I have to get money *soon* or it may have no further use for me."

His perceptions of the people of Monterery are as sharp as those of the Chinese and the Indians. He loved the old city, its ancient Spanish culture, its adobe houses, its windswept sunny beaches, the ocean and the forests. "The town, then, was essentially and wholly

Mexican, and yet almost all the land in the neighbourhood was held by Americans, and it was from the same class, numerically so small, that the principal officials were selected. This Mexican and that Mexican would describe to you his old family estates, not one rood of which remained to him." For, "The Americans had been greedy like designing men," and the Mexicans "curiously unfitted . . . to combat Yankee craft." It is a tragic situation as Stevenson outlines it, and one that he will see in other parts of the world as he travels. "The Monterey of last year [1879] exists no longer. A huge hotel has sprung up in the desert by the railway. . . . Monterey is advertised in the newspapers, and posted in the waiting-rooms at railway stations, as a resort for wealth and fashion. Alas for the little town! It is not strong enough to resist the influence of the flaunting caravanserai, and the poor, quaint, penniless, native gentlemen of Monterey must perish, like a lower race, before the millionaire vulgarians of the Big Bonanza."

And as for Mrs. Osbourne, the people of San Francisco found *Mr.* Osbourne far more charming. There was a general suspicion that she exaggerated his faults. Mrs. Osbourne began to suffer dizzy spells, and then her eyes and her hearing failed. Some kind of neurasthenia from the strain.

In the middle of December Stevenson leaves Monterey for San Francisco. He takes a poor, shabby room at 608 Bush Street. It is the beginning of a lonely period. On the 26th of December he writes Colvin: "For four days I have spoken to no one but my landlady or landlord or to restaurant waiters. This is not a gay way to pass Christmas, is it? and I must own the guts are a little knocked out of me. If I could work, I could worry through better. But I have no style at command for the moment, with the second part of *The Emigrant*, the last of the novel, the essay on Thoreau, and God knows all, waiting for me." Why he hasn't spent Christmas with Fanny is not known. He at first is spending fifty cents a day for dinner, but after a month his finances are so bad that he is forced to cut his dinner allotment to twenty-five cents—a total of forty-five cents a day for all of his meals, even in those times of cheap food not enough for a thin man to live on. "I used to pass as much as that for my first breakfast in the Savile in the grand old palmy days of yore," he writes Baxter, "though the flesh does rebel on occasion."

Nothing seems to go right. He has sent Colvin the first draft of the first part of *The Amateur Emigrant*. Colvin writes Stevenson that, compared to his previous travel papers, it is "but a spiritless record of squalid experiences, little likely to advance his still only half-established reputation." But Stevenson writes back that "*The Emigrant shall be finished.*"

Headaches, problems, troubles on all sides. The Vandergrifts have virtually cut Fanny off, and the Osbournes won't talk to her. Sam Osbourne loses his job, and Stevenson must assume the burden of supporting Fanny and Lloyd and Nellie. Stevenson and his parents barely communicate with each other. His friends in England think he is writing the wrong kind of material in the States. And they are opposed to the forthcoming marriage. Only Bob Stevenson can write: "Live for sensuality! How much our elders deceived us in saying that the pleasures of sense were the most deceptive and fleeting."

Now Stevenson's health gets worse. He has coughing spells, high fever, is unable to speak. Fanny moves him to a hotel in Oakland to care for him, but this is inadequate. After he has a hemorrhage of the lungs, she risks the scandal and moves him into her cottage. They scrape along. Stevenson has asked Baxter to sell off his books. Through his friends, Mrs. Stevenson learns of his illness and recommends that he drink champagne as a tonic. Finally the gravity of the situation strikes the parents, after Fanny, taking the matter into her own hands, writes Colvin, who does not particularly like her. A telegram comes from Stevenson's parents, and he shortly writes Colvin: "My dear people telegraphed me in these words: 'Count on 250 pounds annually.' You may imagine what a blessed business this was."

At last they are married. The date is 19 May, a hot day, cloudy from the smoke of forest fires in the distance. Stevenson and Fanny, too poor to hire a cab, take the ferry across the bay and the cable car to the minister's, a Dr. William A. Scott of St. John's Presbyterian Church. In the records Stevenson is listed as being thirty and single, and Fanny as forty and a "widow." Stevenson could afford only silver wedding rings, and could give Fanny nothing more than a collection of love poems he had been writing over the last six months. A year later Stevenson was to write: "It was not my bliss that I was interested in when I was married; it was sort of a marriage *in extremis*; and if I am where I am, it is thanks to the care of that lady, who married me when I was a mere complication of cough and bones, much fitter for an emblem of mortality than a bridegroom."

❀

So they are married. Sam Osbourne, probably cheered over getting Fanny off his hands, genially arranges a cottage on the grounds of the Hot Springs Hotel in Calistoga for the newlyweds. But it would cost $20 a week and is too elegant for them. A local merchant, a Morris Friedberg, is more helpful. He directs them to a shack in an abandoned gold and silver mine at nearby Silverado, overlooking the Napa Valley. They climb a steep trail to a bunkhouse complex of three tiny cabins. Fanny, who has earned some extensive experience in similar situations in Nevada, works her way through the broken glass, fallen beams, broken crockery, rags and junk and soon has a presentable home for the family (Lloyd has come too). Despite the minor problems (Fanny mashing her thumb while doing repairs, an attack of diphtheria that both Fanny and Lloyd experience, and the general inepitude of some of the local people they would like to count upon

THE SILVERADO SQVATTERS

for help), it seems like a relatively happy time for the newlyweds. Stevenson sets to work, finishing off *The Amateur Emigrant*, doing a draft of *The Silverado Squatters* and revising other pieces he started earlier.

Fanny carries on a correspondence with her as yet unmet mother-in-law about her new husband, smoothing over a lifetime of wounds between her Louis and his parents, with constant references to "my dear boy." "Taking care of Louis is, as you must know, very like angling for shy trout; one must understand when to pay out the line, and exercise the greatest caution in drawing him in." Stevenson was obviously content; he would sit on the mine platform and entertain people who came to see them—Belle and Joe Strong, Fanny's sister Nellie, Virgil and Dora Williams. They ate wild duck and venison. Belle remarked that "the change in Louis was amazing; he was like a different man." Joe Strong drew a sketch of the Stevensons in their mining camp: both hard at work with writing pads on their laps, Fanny on a chair, Stevenson in bed. Stevenson's parents had made several requests to Fanny to come to Scotland. In the middle of July she was sufficiently confident of her husband's health to write Mrs. Stevenson: "Now, at last, I think he may venture to make the journey without fear, though every step must be made cautiously. I am sure now that he is on the high road to recovery and health, and I believe his best medicine will be the meeting with you and his father, for whom he pines like a child. I have had a sad time through it all, but it has been worse for you, I know." So, with Lloyd, the Stevensons cross America by first-class Pullman in an uneventful trip—which produces not a word of copy for Stevenson—and embark first class on the *City*

Married at last, Stevenson and Fanny take up residence in an abandoned miner's shanty at Silverado. Somewhere out of the picture, which was done by Fanny's son-in-law, Joe Strong, is her son Lloyd. A crowded honeymoon!

of Chester on 7 August, 1880, a year to the day after Stevenson had set off on the *Devonia*.

"Stevenson returned from America," wrote an English critic, "with some admirable travel sketches, a fading middle-aged woman and tuberculosis." Colvin met the Stevensons at Liverpool, where the ship docked. He expected to serve as a buffer between Stevenson and his father, but Fanny, it seems, was determined to establish peace with the parents so that her husband could go about the business of writing without the continual feuding that had been his lot so far. Instead of battling Thomas Stevenson she agreed with him, so he thought, and the two became close friends. Margaret Stevenson was not much older than she, and the two women got along very well, particularly on the question of Louis's well-being and his writing.

It was Stevenson's own circle of friends that resented Fanny—Henley and Colvin in particular. The friends resented Fanny for various reasons, one being that she was so protective of her husband. They resented her as an outsider, as an American, as a woman, as a person with her own ideas which they did not want to respect. As well as the doctors she knew the precariousness of her husband's health, having nursed him over and over again. She had seen him weak, tired, nervous, depressed, anxious, spitting blood, his eyes failing, teeth rotting, lungs gasping. She tried to enforce regular hours, to put people out at sensible times. In short, to keep him alive. A doctor in Edinburgh suggests Davos, Swiss resort of well-to-do consumptives. They set off, stopping at London. Friends take over.

Fanny to Mrs. Stevenson: "If we do not get away soon from London, I shall become an embittered woman. It is not good for my mind, or my body either, to sit smiling at Louis's friends until I feel like a hypocritical Cheshire cat, talking stiff nothings with one and another in order to let Louis have a chance with the one he cares most for, and all the time furtively watching the clock and thirsting for their blood

In Davos, Stevenson and his stepson, Lloyd, collaborated on a number of penny printing projects. Stevenson did wood blocks, like this one of Lord Nelson and the Tar, and wrote simple verses, and Lloyd ran them off on his hand press.

because they stay so late." It turned out to be a kind of war, the hard-drinking people like Henley demanding Stevenson follow a Bohemian life, and Fanny trying to preserve what health there might be left in her husband. But, eventually, the law is laid down. No one with a cold is allowed to enter their rooms. Fanny rules. Female tyranny over our good friend, say the friends. Immediately Henley appears with a heavy cold which he passes on to Stevenson, who then becomes seriously ill.

Eventually they reach Davos—clear air, high mountains—in November, 1880. They will stay until the following April.

A monotonous, healthful life. Most of the patients are English. A few die, others pester Stevenson, a young lady tries to convert him . . . There is an English writer he can talk to, Addington Symonds, who writes home that Stevenson is "a very interesting man . . . really clever . . . a great acquisition." Stevenson has less to say about Symonds.

The snow falls. The crisp air at first helps Stevenson, but then he falls ill. Fanny is directly affected by the high altitude. It is the first step of a lifetime search the couple are to take for the perfect place that will satisfy the health needs of both. More snow. Picturesque. But Stevenson loses much of the benefits of his first season at Davos with illness and the fruitless pursuit of a history of the Scottish highlands from 1715, a project most strongly urged upon him by his father. But he produces some essays. Whatever benefits he has gained from Davos are lost in a summer in Scotland with his parents; the climate of his native land has never agreed with him, yet he works doggedly, turning out some short stories—what he calls "crawlers" and Fanny "ghost stories," one of them being a piece known as the "Body-Snatcher."

One day Stevenson notices Lloyd drawing a map of a fanciful island to entertain himself. Stevenson begins to spin a story about the island and its pirate treasure, and Thomas Stevenson is drawn into it. Suddenly a full-blown book is in the offing. Thomas Stevenson spends the day making up a list of the contents of Billy Bones's chest. "My father," wrote Stevenson in an article about the genesis of his first popular book, "caught fire at once with all the romance and childishness of his original nature. His own stories, that every night of his life he put himself to sleep with, dealt perpetually with ships, roadside inns, robbers, old sailors, and commercial travellers before the era of steam."

Stevenson wrote a chapter a day that summer in Scotland. However, the book was not finished when he went to London in the fall. Meanwhile a certain Dr. Japp, a Scottish pedant, who went to chide

Stevenson about some errors in his essay on Thoreau, instead became interested in the book, then called *The Sea Cook,* and took the early chapters away to give them to a friend of his who edited a magazine called *Young Folks.*

Stevenson is also absorbed in fruitless pursuit: He has conceived the strange idea of applying for the post of Professor of History and Constitutional Law at the University of Edinburgh. He makes a tremendous effort to enlist the support of his closest friends, getting testimonials from fourteen about his qualifications. But when the final decision is made, Stevenson has only nine votes out of several hundred. The post would have paid him £250 per year, without a great demand on his time, yet it is hardly the kind of work he is interested in.

Back to Davos they go again, arriving on 18 October. Now they take a small house, the Châlet am Stein, amidst the snows. But the health that Stevenson seeks somehow escapes him. A few weeks later Symonds, who has remained at Davos, writes a friend about Stevenson: "He was lying, ghastly, in bed—purple cheekbones, yellow cheeks, bloodless lips—fever all over him—without appetite—and all about him so utterly forlorn. 'Woggs' [their dog] squealing. Mrs. Stevenson doing her best to make things comfortable." Later in the month Symonds reported that Stevenson was better "but he lost blood a few nights since." Meanwhile Fanny was suffering from gallstones, and in December she goes, with Lloyd, to Berne. The dog has an infection. Symonds writes his friend: "I wish to goodness we were all like Stevenson! To be reasonable and justly self-satisfied about one's style, to take life smoothly, and have a cheerful conscience! oh, what bliss!"

Despite all the health problems, Stevenson, so he said, "sat down one morning to the unfinished tale" of *The Sea Cook,* and in a "second tide of delighted industry" completed the novel at the rate of a chap-

Treasure Island

ter a day. *The Sea Cook* brought him £34 7s 6d as a serial in *Young Folks*. Since it was such a departure from his other writing, Stevenson put the dramatic byline "Captain George North" on it, in a sense expressing another side of his personality. The readers expressed boredom, for they wanted a different type of work. His friends thought the work beneath him. It was not until it appeared as a bound book under the title of *Treasure Island*, with Stevenson's name on it, that the public—adult mainly—took it up and made him famous.

By April, 1882, Stevenson not only had the finished manuscripts of *The Sea Cook* and *The Silverado Squatters* and ninety pages of magazine work and some other material, but some poems for children which were eventually to appear as *A Child's Garden of Verses*. It was a productive year, and the quality of his material was high. Then back to Scotland and a visit with his parents. A bad summer, for work and health. Raw winds, cold rains, hemorrhages, a gallstone for Fanny. The London specialist that Stevenson had been consulting agreed that a third winter in Davos was not advisable, so to the south of France Stevenson went, taking along cousin Bob.

In Montpellier, where he finds prices too high for his income, he has a hemorrhage. The doctor advises Marseille—cheaper, further east. He takes a house in a Marseille suburb, smack in the path of the notorious mistral winds. Fanny comes in October. In December they decide they must move because there is an outbreak of typhoid. To Nice and Hyères they go, in search of the right house, the right climate, the right place to live and work. Hyères seems ideal. In May, 1883, Stevenson has a bad hemorrhage. But some progress has been made. *Century* magazine has bought *The Silverado Squatters* as a serial for £40. He receives an advance of £100 for the book rights to *Treasure Island* (though by the end of the century only 75,000 copies have been sold, despite its great acclaim among the adult world; many of its editions are pirated and bring no royalties). He writes another serial for *Young Folks*, this one called *The Black Arrow*, inferior in quality to *Treasure Island* but a critical success with the readers. *Prince Otto* is under way, and *A Child's Garden of Verses* collects more poems.

The annual trip to Scotland, with its promise of chills, winds and hemorrhages is somehow avoided, and the Thomas Stevensons instead come to France. Robert Louis is earning "more" money this year—his income will total £465—and he feels a great feeling of confidence in facing his father. Thomas Stevenson, it must be said, is getting elderly. A little weak, senile. Quarreling is no longer his forte. Henley and Baxter make an excursion to Nice—bad news for Fanny, because the all-night drinking parties lay Stevenson low. They finally depart, leaving Stevenson down with a bad lung and a kidney infection.

The English doctor at Nice warns that Stevenson might be dying. Fanny calls for help, to Simpson, who does not come; to Bob, who does.

Stevenson is a mess. This is the second major breakdown of his life, the first being the incident in the mountains in California. When he is returned to Hyères his right arm is strapped to his side and he is under orders not to exert himself. No talking. So he scribbles notes. He develops sciatica, rheumatism, opthalmia. He cannot speak, read, move. He lies in a restless state all day until drugged at night. When possible, he writes with his left hand, turning out a few more poems for the *Garden*. One night in May he awakes in a fit of coughing, blood oozing from his mouth. A message, providentially already written, is at his side: "Don't be frightened. If this is death, it is quite easy." Fanny is shaken, too shaken to spoon out his ergotin, so Stevenson himself measures out the dose of medicine.

The doctor is sent from England to examine the dying man. He writes about Stevenson: "He must be perfectly tranquil, trouble about nothing, have no shocks or surprises, not even pleasant ones; must not eat too much, drink too much, laugh too much; may write a little, but not too much; talk *very* little, and walk no more than can be helped."

Aside from this morbid opinion, Lloyd Osbourne, who had been away at school for over a year, offers another view when he returns to his mother and stepfather: "The routine of his existence suited him to perfection—at his desk all the morning; then luncheon, with an excellent *vin du pays*, and never lacking a salad; a stroll afterward in the sunshine, to drop in and talk politics with old Le Roux, the wine-merchant, or to have a chat with his friend Powell, the English chemist. Then home to look over his correspondence and write a few letters, with an excellent little dinner to follow and a conversation shared by Valentine, our vivacious cook and maid of all work. . . .

"Stevenson offers the fascinating study of a man whose spiritual concentration kept him alive. He simply wouldn't die; refused to; and those who would have him different would not now be reading his books—because there would have been no books. . . . First there was this tremendous prepossession for his work, and secondly, his invincible refusal to become an invalid. He was never willing to coddle himself, or to acquiesce in illness if he could possibly avoid doing so."

Fanny reads the *Lancet*, a British medical publication aimed at doctors, not nonmedical people. Alarming news! Vinegar is discovered to be full of perils; salads carry the eggs of tapeworms; salt hardens the arteries and shortens one's life. Cholera breaks out in Hyères. There is danger everywhere. They go back to England, an ailing wife, near-dead husband.

Lloyd: "I often think it was a mistake he ever left Hyères; it was so entirely congenial and suited him so well. . . . [My mother] fell into a panic . . . absurd."

✿

They settle in Bournemouth, a seaside town, in a rented house. Stevenson remains ill, money is short and he must ask his parents for help. But work progresses despite his illnesses. Visits from friends from London (with colds). Fanny is vexed. Better sales, book contracts. In the spring Mr. Thomas Stevenson surprisingly gives Fanny a house in Bournemouth, along with £500 for furnishings and decorations—a pleasant surprise. It is set on an acre and a half, is neat and trim. The vicar calls on the Stevensons. Respectability, dullness and similar vilas stretch for miles in every direction. Stevenson names the house Skerryvore, in honor of a lighthouse his father had built in Scotland years back. Lloyd: "In his heart I doubt if he really ever liked 'Skerryvore'; he never spoke of it with regret; left it with no apparent pang. The Victorianism it exemplified was jarring to every feeling he possessed."

Stevenson is a virtual prisoner in the house, though he makes some escapes to London, Paris, Exeter. But invariably he returns the worse in health. Life is a series of relapses and recoveries. Lloyd: "His health throughout was at its lowest ebb; never was he so spectral, so emanciated, so unkempt and tragic a figure."

His collaboration with Henley continues. *Deacon Brodie* is a mild success on the stage (but the only one). They forge ahead with *Admiral Guinea, Beau Austin* and *Macaire*; they have outlines for a dozen others that are never tried, probably fortunately, for the team is not theatrically-minded and the time they invest is wasted. The older Stevensons come to Bournemouth later in the year, taking separate lodgings. Thomas Stevenson is failing in health. It is not a happy time for anyone, but Robert Louis continues to work doggedly, productively, relentlessly.

He has a dream, a nightmare, awaking one gray morning in 1885 with three of the scenes in what is to be *The Strange Case of Dr. Jekyll and Mr. Hyde.* He has dreamed the scenes in considerable detail, and he dashes them off at white heat. "In the small hours of the morning," says Fanny later, "I was awakened by cries of horror from Louis. Thinking he had a nightmare, I awakened him. He said angrily: 'Why did you wake me? I was dreaming a fine bogey tale.' I had awakened him at the first transformation scene."

Stevenson liked to pretend that many of his ideas, in fact complete stories, came out of his dreams through the auspices of the "little people." He worked at *Dr. Jekyll* almost in a trance, turning out some twenty-five thousand words (so the legend goes) in three days, a prodigious task. Fanny does not like the story, which it seems is still a draft. Lloyd: "He read it aloud to my mother and myself. . . . I listened to it spellbound. Stevenson, who had a voice an actor might have envied, read it with an intensity that made shivers run up and down my spine." But Fanny does not like it. "Stevenson was beside himself with anger. He trembled; his hand shook on the manuscript." Stevenson burns the manuscript, either in annoyance at Fanny or in order not to have the first version influence the new story rapidly forming in his mind. Another three days' work, another twenty-five thousand words (so the same legend), though all the biographers question the ability of a sick man hemorrhaging at the lungs to write eight thousand words a day, a task almost physically impossible even for a heroically well man. At any rate, *The Strange Case of Dr. Jekyll and Mr. Hyde* is soon to become one of our language's minor classics.

There are loose ends in this story of good and evil. Logically it does not hold together. It is a kind of fantasy, a morality story of good and evil; some of the facts are distorted. Nevertheless the grand symbolism of a good man releasing the evil in himself and thereby becoming another person is the theme that captures the reader. The story sells forty thousand copies in six months. It influences other writers, among them Oscar Wilde (in *The Story of Dorian Gray*) and helps set the London mood of Sir Arthur Conan Doyle's Sherlock Holmes stories. Though *Dr. Jekyll* was an instant success with the public, it was a critical failure. But it brought Stevenson money when, as usual, he desperately needed it. "I drive on with Jekyll, bankruptcy at my heels." Unfortunately the book was widely pirated in America, where some quarter of a million copies were sold without any royalties for the author.

This entire period at Skerryvore, which ended in the late spring of 1887, was one of almost unrelieved physical suffering. Lloyd, who of all the people around Stevenson probably concealed less and wrote the most objectively and clearly, said about these years: "He had horrifying hemorrhages, long spells when he was doomed to lie motionless on his bed lest the slightest movement should restart the flow, when he would speak in whispers, and one sat beside him and tried to be entertaining—in that room he was only too likely to leave in his coffin.

"How thus handicapped he wrote his books is one of the marvels of literature—books so robustly and aboundingly alive that it is incredible that they came out of a sick-room; and such well-sustained books with no slowing down of their original impetus, nor the least suggestion of those intermissions when their author lay at the point of death." During this period Stevenson wrote not only *Dr. Jekyll* but *Kidnapped*, the series of plays, many of his best short stories, published *A Child's Garden of Verses*, *The Merry Men* and many others.

Then another turning point comes. It is April, 1887. Thomas Stevenson seems to be dying. He longs to return to Edinburgh. His mind falters, though his body is moderately active and he is still able to walk. He is brought home in a railway ambulance, dying there on 7 May. Notified by telegram, Stevenson goes to Edinburgh but is too ill himself to attend the funeral. Life takes a strange twist. The doctors in Edinburgh, fearing for Stevenson's own life, say he cannot return to Skerryvore. He must go to Colorado!

Fanny is brokenhearted! "Life has been too happy in Skerryvore,"

she writes Lloyd, "the envying gods had struck it down." Strange statement.

But not even Colorado is ahead.

＊

Sam Osbourne, the elder. We have lost sight of him (as everyone soon will). One evening, as he is about to go off to his incredibly boring job as court reporter at the night session, he asks his second wife, Paulie, to have midnight supper with him when he comes home. An unusual

request, for usually he eats alone. Or doesn't come home so early. Sam
kisses her goodbye, goes off down the street whistling.

Disappears.

Headlines in the newspapers: "Prominent Legal Aide," etc.

Not a clue.

So long, Sam.

Years later someone tells Fanny that Sam has been seen in South
Africa.

Not interested.

But young Lloyd was shaken up.

*

The death of his father meant another major turn in Stevenson's life.
He was now in his thirty-seventh year, and to this time he had been
dependent on his father for financial aid, even though his own income
had been rising. His father's death was to free him, though he inherited no money directly from his father, despite rumors about the vast
sums of money he was said to have been left. Four years earlier
Thomas Stevenson had restored his son to his will. Under the new
terms, Margaret Stevenson's marriage settlement, some three thousand
pounds, went directly to her son when her husband died; she received
the £26,000 of her husband's estate. With the small sum of money he
received, Stevenson was for the moment, at least, free from financial
worries, though the standard of living he and Fanny adopted soon put
him into wobbly financial straits. But with the new money he made
the fortuitous move that put him into direct contact with the real
sources of money: the American publishers.

The Stevensons decided to go to America, rather innocently, not
knowing of the gold mine that lay ahead. They booked passage with
Lloyd and Mrs. Margaret Stevenson and the French maid, Valentine
Roche, they had picked up in Hyères, on a ship called the *Ludgate*

A rare photograph of Stevenson, discovered by Lloyd Osbourne's first wife, Katharine Durham.

When Stevenson was living in Bournemouth, the American painter John Singer Sargent visited him and painted two large portraits, the second one including Fanny.

Hill. They discovered after they boarded her that the cargo was "monkeys, stallions, cows, matches, hay." A smelly ship. But: "I was so happy on board that ship, I could not have believed it possible," Stevenson wrote Bob a month later. "I had literally forgotten what happiness was. And the full mind—full of externals and physical things, not of cares and labours and rot about a fellow's behavior. My heart literally sang."

When the *Ludgate Hill* arrived in New York the Stevensons found that they were welcomed by a crowd of admirers and reporters. It was a startling event. Lightweight interviews followed: "The cor-

A photograph taken at Bournemouth shows Stevenson in almost the same pose as the Sargent painting, but more pensive and less animated.

rect pronunciation of Jekyll is Jeekyll," Stevenson is quoted as saying. Another reporter wrote: "Mr. Stevenson has a classic head from which proceeds a hacking cough." He had caught the cold as the ship approached the States. Stevenson wrote Colvin that "the poor interviewer lads pleased me," though "my reception here was idiotic to the last degree."

He had arrived in a land of pirates. His works had been stolen by one publisher after another. All he had on his arrival was fame of a kind he had not received in England. Along with the reporters who greeted him aboard ship were Will Low and the editor of *Scribner's*, then a leading American magazine. *The Strange Case of Dr. Jekyll and Mr. Hyde*, which had already had a successful run as a play in Boston, was about to open in New York. Stevenson was taken to a press party at a hotel on Broadway. He gave interviews, suggested that the public buy the legal editions of his works and not the pirated ones, said a good word for President Grover Cleveland but added, "I am not in love with any form of government," and finally escaped to bed to nurse his cold. Some friends took him to Newport where he spent a few days in bed recovering his health.

In New York he was besieged with offers. *Scribner's* offered $3,500 for twelve articles on any subject Stevenson might want to write about. Sam McClure, the publisher of the *New York World*, then a dynamic daily newspaper, offered $10,000 a year for a weekly column. Stevenson had trouble translating dollars into pounds; he thought he was being overpaid, felt he couldn't write so much on order, and refused. But McClure bought *The Black Arrow* at a high price. It is hard to equate these figures in today's terms, considering the rate of inflation. You might multiply them by ten or twenty. Then, in his naïveté, not having his friends Colvin, Baxter and Henley to advise him, Stevenson agreed to the same contract with McClure, for his next novel, that he had already signed for with *Scribner's*. Embar-

The Wrong Box

rassment. He had to apologize all around and wiggle out graciously. But, no hard feelings. The great author can do no wrong. Apologies and smiles. Capital fellow, that Stevenson with the hacking cough.

And now, off to Lake Saranac, America's answer to Davos, discovered five years earlier by Dr. Edward L. Trudeau for the care of the tubercular. Here Stevenson settles down to a long, dull, cold winter, while the rest of his party wander about America, returning to Saranac from time to time to see the ailing writer and to check on his work, worry about his health.

Left alone with Lloyd and the French maid, Stevenson does little but work on *The Master of Ballantrae* and take short walks in the

"Get out!" snaps Stevenson, as Lloyd unexpectedly pops into his study with his camera.

bitter cold. His health is tolerable. He works at his monthly essays for *Scribner's* and slides into a collaboration with Lloyd on a novel, *The Wrong Box*, one of several such works he was to engage upon with his stepson.

And then a curious situation arises, one that comes close to splintering Stevenson's tight little world. It involves four people: Stevenson, Fanny, Henley and Stevenson's cousin, Katherine de Mattos. The core of it lies in the ancient antagonism between Fanny and Henley, which is active on Henley's part since he had deeply resented her role in Stevenson's life and had objected to the marriage; less active on hers, for apparently she had little objection to Henley except when his drinking bouts and late hours when the two were together seriously affected her husband's health. Henley resented Stevenson being three thousand miles away—due solely, he felt, to Fanny's overbearing control. There was possibly a certain amount of jingoism and male chauvinism involved: an English *man* as opposed to an American woman.

The running tension came to a head in March, 1888, over a short story that had originated with Katherine de Mattos and was taken over by Fanny. Mrs. de Mattos had written a brief piece about meeting a girl who escapes from a madhouse, but she had been unsuccessful in selling it. Fanny liked the idea but thought the girl should be fantasized into a "nixie," a kind of spirit. Mrs. de Mattos politely disagreed. Then—in Henley's presence—Fanny offered the opinion that since Henley had tried to place the story with a publication but had failed, she be allowed to rewrite the story according to her own version. Mrs. de Mattos agreed in a manner that (to Henley) clearly meant, "I wish you wouldn't." Fanny, being obstinate, American and a woman, went ahead with her idea, using much of Mrs. de Mattos' material, then sent it to *Scribner's* (to which her husband was now a contributer). The story was accepted and published under her own byline, without any credit to Mrs. de Mattos. Fanny also kept the payment.

Eventually Henley saw the issue containing "The Nixie," and in a roundabout manner, in a long, depressed letter to Stevenson full of complaints about his own life, mentioned "The Nixie" and Fanny in a critical way, wondering, asking, pointing out, that it was Katherine's and why wasn't there at least a joint signature? It was a shock for Stevenson to receive a letter from one of his closest friends accusing his wife of plagiarism. He immediately wrote to Fanny, not quoting Henley in full. Fanny at the time was in San Francisco, facing an operation for cancer of the throat. At the same time, Stevenson wrote a pompously stiff letter to Henley, starting with, "I write with indescribable difficulty; and if not with perfect temper, you are to remember how very rarely a husband is expected to receive such accusations

A portrait of Stevenson painted at Vailima by Count Guglielmo Nerli, an Italian artist on an around-the-world tour. Fanny disliked it; she said the artist tried too hard.

against his wife." The situation got worse: Stevenson hoped for some kind of apology from Henley to Fanny; Henley could not retract, but wrote back that "I shall never cease from regretting that I gave you this useless, this unnecessary pain." Henley had not retracted as far as Fanny was concerned; he was sorry for hurting Stevenson, his friend. Meanwhile Katherine de Mattos wrote Stevenson a letter, rather carefully worded, in which she said that she had not asked Henley to intervene, had now refused him permission to go further in the matter. But she made it clear that her version of the story was written before Fanny's. "I trust this matter is not making you feel as ill as all of us," she said in conclusion. Of all the people involved, it was Stevenson, the most "innocent" in the situation, who, his friends felt, suffered the most.

The quarrel was to drag on. Fanny underwent the operation, which indicated no cancerous growth. Stevenson fell into a deep state of depression, which some people believe led him dangerously close to suicide; it was a mood that was to last well into his coming voyage to the Pacific. From San Francisco Fanny wrote to Baxter concerning her husband's will. In it both Henley and Katherine were mentioned and were to receive modest sums. "Already the hands that dealt me the cruellest blow are held out to be filled," she said. "I am not likely to change my feelings of resentment. The wrong can never be condoned, nor do I ever wish to see England again. It is most probable that I never shall. Every penny that goes to them, any of them, goes with my bitterest ill will."

*

Why did Fanny "steal" Katherine's story? Did she misunderstand a forced assent, so subtle that it eluded her insensitive ears? Much later she wrote in her diary a passage that bears upon the situation, expressing her yearning to be much more than just an appendage to her famous husband, to be an independent person, not being forced to rely upon someone else for her food and clothes. The passage was deleted from the manuscript and parts of it so heavily inked over that they are not decipherable. Some of the crucial thoughts read: "I wish I were able to write a little tale that I might have some money of my own. I know that people speak about my [eight words inked out]." She then mentions giving away money that she has earned to other people. "I wonder what would become of a man, and to what he would degenerate, if his life was that of a woman's: to get the 'run of her teeth' and presents of her clothes, and supposed to be always under the bonds of the deepest gratitude for any further sums. I would work very hard to earn a couple of pounds a month, and then I could easily earn much more, but there is my position as Louis's wife, therefore I cannot."

❀

Fanny meets Sam Osbourne's "widowed" Pauline. "Paulie was very much like Fanny," is the general comment. Sam chose a wife as much as Fanny as he could find, people say. Fanny and Paulie become good friends. An Osbourne niece: "While Aunt P. was sweeter, she lacked the keen-mindedness of Aunt Fan and then her deafness must have been a trial to both of them." Fanny and Paulie have something in common: that bastard Sam. Paulie pours out her troubles to Fanny. Fanny knows them all. Nothing new in the recounting. But she *understands*. Genial Sam. The bastard.

❀

The Stevensons help out the poor "widow," secretly, financially. At the time of the disappearance Stevenson sends her funds through Lloyd. Now Fanny helps out. "Just in case of an emergency . . ."

Stevenson has a lifelong history of helping out people, some of them unknown. A generous, bad trait. The extent of his generosities has never been known.

THE SOUTH SEAS

NOW it is April; the snows melt, the slush is knee deep, the waters drip from the eaves, the spring sun shines brightly. But Stevenson's soul is dark. Gloomily he packs up with Lloyd, his mother and Valentine, goes to New York (a visit with Mark Twain, both men sitting on a bench in Washington Square). Stevenson finds the thrifty Hotel St. Stephen too dismal. Will Low recommends a place in Manasquan, on the New Jersey coast. Meanwhile . . .

Fanny, in good health, energy overflowing, has thrown herself into an often-discussed project: finding a boat the family can take for a prolonged cruise. This and that place have been discussed. The Greek isles, God knows what. Fanny, in San Francisco, finds a luxury yacht, the *Casco*, $500 a month, plus crew, plus this and that. Total, $750. Two thousand of Stevenson's three thousand pounds are to go rapidly, but meanwhile there is all that new money from the American publishers. No need to worry about the future: The future is now. They spend wildly. To Stevenson, idling in Manasquan, a telegram comes:

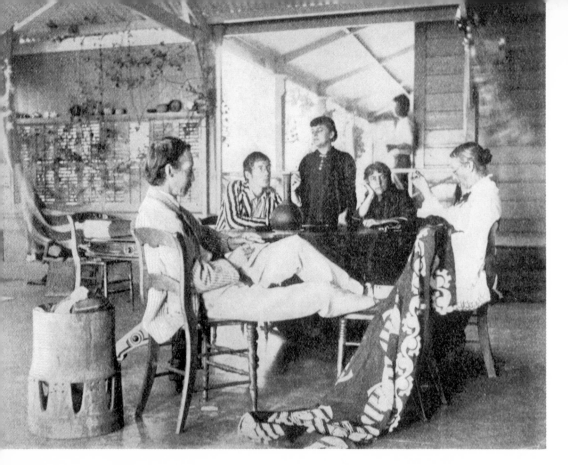

The Stevensons took easily to the relaxed life of the tropics, and as they advanced further into it shed more and more of their European customs and took up local ones. The young man in the striped jacket is Lloyd; standing next to him is Belle; seated with her head on her hand is Fanny, and sewing a bolt of printed cloth is Margaret Stevenson.

CAN SECURE SPLENDID SEA-GOING SCHOONER YACHT CASCO FOR SEVEN HUNDRED AND FIFTY A MONTH WITH MOST COMFORTABLE ACCOMMODATION FOR SIX AFT AND SIX FORWARD? CAN BE READY FOR SEA IN TEN DAYS. REPLY IMMEDIATELY. FANNY.

The telegraph boy stands expectantly. Stevenson dashes off a reply, tips him:

BLESSED GIRL, TAKE THE YACHT AND EXPECT US IN TEN DAYS.

The owner of the yacht has insisted that the Stevensons take his normal crew, which includes one Captain Otis, a crusty old sea dog who has a sailor's dislike of landlubbers. One look at disheveled, sallow-skinned, untidy, frail R.L.S. and the captain quietly orders sea-burial equipment stowed aboard. No fool, this old sea dog. Be prepared. Meanwhile Fanny, with a real project on her mind, has been busy in the markets—five in the family, five in the crew, seven days a week for six months. A lot of food has to be bought and brought aboard, put in the hold in logical order. Barrels of flour and sugar, sacks of rice and beans, butter, lard, syrup, dried beef, hams, bacon, dried and canned fruit, tobacco and cigarette paper, coal and kerosene, all kinds of beverages, and hundreds of volumes of reading matter, for everyone is a heavy reader.

Now it is 28 June, 1888. Dawn breaks over the bay. The *Casco* is gentled eased seaward by a tug, and Stevenson enters the last great phase of his life.

The first three days are a surprise. Only Lloyd and his stepfather are about. Everyone else, including Captain Otis, is kept below with a touch of queasy stomach.

Captain Otis, it is learned later, has the reputation of having a "complete contempt for his passengers and employers." It is not quite a happy ship. Stevenson and his mother, presumably drawing upon the heritage of lighthouse building, turn out to be good sailors; the rest of the passengers barely get their sea legs, leave the dead lights open (so that the yacht ships water in squalls). Fanny talks to the helmsman, irritating Otis. Thirty days out of San Francisco they land in the Marquesas. Fanny writes Mrs. Sitwell about "hating and fearing the sea." Stevenson, on the other hand, says he loves the sea and sailing, and believes his health is improving on this vast ocean. And now land is sighted:

"The first experience can never be repeated. The first love, the first sunrise, the first South Sea island, are memories apart, and touch a virginity of sense." Suddenly the islands appear out of the early morning darkness on the horizon; the first rays of the sun pick up a mountain peak, the land heaves up before them.

They creep along the shore. The anchor is dropped in a bay, a canoe comes out, and another and more, and suddenly the ship is swarming with islanders. "I was now escaped out of the shadow of the Roman empire, under whose toppling monuments we were all cradled, whose laws and letters are on every hand of us, constraining and preventing. I was not to see what men might be whose fathers had never studied Virgil, had never been conquered by Caesar, and never been ruled by the wisdom of Gaius or Papinian."

From the South Seas Stevenson will write a series of reports for the *New York Sun*. They have been criticized for not being "popular," yet Stevenson was delving into completely unfamiliar material, seizing the essence, and putting it into clear, graphic terms. It was a kind of popular anthropology, and of a perception far better than many professional anthropologists, then and now. Yet his material was never boring. A constant preoccupation was the conflict between island ways and those of the West. He wrote about cannibalism, for example, from the point of view of the islander, but without apologizing for it. He could see how a great chief could feel insulted and angry at off-hand Western ways, how the whites would wonder why a Kanaka would fail to understand *their* ways while at the same time making no effort to understand his. He wrote with great emotion about an islander whose sacred stones—pagan to the Christian missionaries—were destroyed in the name of Christianity, which he did not understand, and then was arrested for desecrating the mission cemetery; the man could not see the difference between one act of destruction and the other. The white in all his horror stood out starkly in the Pacific. In another instance two old chiefs, cannibals by tradition, are put

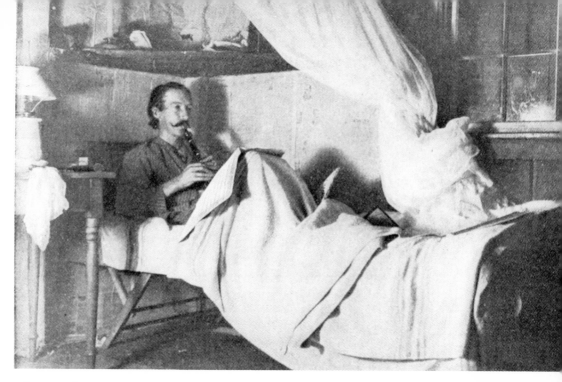

Wherever he went, Stevenson took along a small flute, which he liked to play in bed (he wrote and read in bed, too). He was not much of a musician, but he enjoyed his simple melodies.

below a bridge while a young girl defecates upon them by order of the civilized whites. It was to be like this throughout the Pacific, and when Stevenson found himself taking sides, it was invariably with the brown-skinned man, not the white.

In the Marquesas Stevenson soon makes friends with the islanders, though at first, as he readily admits, he is extremely nervous about their menacing appearance. "There could be nothing more natural than these apprehensions," he wrote for the *Sun*, "nor anything more groundless." He believed the people culturally similar to the Scottish highlanders of the eighteenth century, and he would tell them stories from his own heritage, which they enjoyed. He made friends everywhere, and when the *Casco* left for Tahiti in September, it was with regret on both sides.

At Tahiti Stevenson comes down with a "fever" and a cough. The party moves onward in search of a place where he can recuperate.

They leave Papeete, the main town of Tahiti, and skirt the island, landing at a place called Taravao, sailing through dangerous reefs. Taravao is on the south shore of the island, so remote from Papeete that it seems like another world. But this tiny hamlet with its malarial mists does not suit the Stevensons. They hear of a more suitable place across the island, and hire a horse and wagon from a Chinese trader.

Meanwhile Captain Otis has found that his jibboom is damaged. He repairs it, and sails around to the other side, where the Stevensons are settled in a house belonging to the chief's daughter, Princess Moë. Stevenson has a bad fever; he is nursed back to health by the Princess. Several weeks go by before Stevenson is well enough to continue. The older Mrs. Stevenson invites some of her newfound friends among the village women aboard ship; there is a feast, followed by a prayer in thanks for Stevenson's recovery. The ill-tempered Captain Otis, in annoyance, strikes the goddam mast with his goddam fist. The goddam mast crumbles. Dry rot. Crisis. Otis deposits his passengers on shore and sails off to Papeete for a new mast. The port is only a few miles away on the map, but it is reached through dangerous channels, of the sea and the mind. The party expects Otis back in a few days with a new mast. Meanwhile Stevenson settles down to his current project, *The Master of Ballantrae*, which is near completion.

The days go by . . . weeks. They have been virtually adopted by Princess Moë's father, Chief Ori, who honors Stevenson by exchanging names with him, the Chief becoming Rui (that is, Louis) and Stevenson Teriitera, the Chief's formal name. Now the weeks become a month, two. The supplies Otis has left with them are used up, and Ori-Rui feeds them from his own larder. But the foreigners, unwillingly, are making demands he can no longer meet. So the Chief makes a dangerous trip by whaleboat to Papeete for supplies. Ori, too, seems lost in the maelstrom. At last he returns, with provisions from the *Casco*, and money, and a letter from Otis and a basket of champagne.

Three days before Christmas the *Casco* arrives and takes off the Stevenson party, amid sad farewells. On the twenty-fifth they leave Papeete for Honolulu, running through a heavy storm, to find that they had been given up for lost. The *Casco* is dismissed, a fortune gone with not much use of the yacht, and the Stevensons settled down in Honolulu, lately an island empire, now the burgeoning city of an expanding colonial America.

The Master of Ballantrae is finished, and Stevenson takes some time off to explore the islands. His stepdaughter Belle and her husband Joe Strong have been living in Honolulu, and they introduce him to the island's last king, Kalakua. Stevenson visits the leper colony founded by the famed Father Damien on Molokai; Damien had died the year before the Stevensons arrived. Stevenson thought of writing an extended report on missionaries in the Pacific, of which he had little actual knowledge. His own excursion into this area was a defense of Father Damien, who had been the object of a rather unfair letter by a Protestant missionary. Dr. Hyde, the missionary, called Damien "a coarse, dirty man, headstrong and bigoted. . . . He was not a pure man in his relations with women, and the leprosy of which he died should have been attributed to his own vices and carelessness." Stevenson wrote an extended reply, which, as he boasted at the time, was openly libelous of Hyde. The controversy broke into the international press. Hyde could have sued for libel, but fortunately for Stevenson he dismissed him as a "bohemian crank."

Now comes another trip, this time on the American ship *Equator*, a trading schooner. The party consists of Stevenson, Fanny, Joe Strong and Lloyd. They visit various islands, with various colorful experience (hostile natives in one place, drunken natives in another, a murderous king on still another island), all furnishing material for Stevenson's newspaper columns. The trip is rough, for Stevenson writes his mother, now in Scotland: "Fanny has stood the hardships of this rough cruise

When the Stevensons came ashore on Upolu, the island was undeveloped and torn by local wars. The drawing is by Belle; Teuila is her Samoan name.

wonderfully; but I do not think I could enforce her to another of the same. I've been first rate, though I am now done for lack of green food. Joe is, I fear, really ill; and Lloyd has sores on his legs." (Yet he was to persuade Fanny to still another cruise.)

The *Equator* stops at Samoa. Stevenson's first impression is that these are not particularly appealing islands. He is interested in a recent native war, a description of which was intended as the conclusion of *In the South Seas.* The material will eventually become a separate work, *A Footnote to History.* But despite the poor impression of Samoa, they go ashore at the tiny town of Apia on the island of Upolu. Up to this point the Stevensons had vague plans of working their way around the world via Sydney, Ceylon, the Suez Canal and Marseille, arriving in England in June, 1890.

But there is a change of plans. On 2 December, 1889, Stevenson writes to Colvin: "I am minded not to stay very long in Samoa," but seven weeks later he writes surprisingly to a friend, Lady Taylor, that he was the owner of an estate on Upolu. He plans on coming to England to break up his establishment. But he was never to see his own country again. Eventually Lloyd went to Bournemouth and to Scotland to sell off Skerryvore and to tie up Stevenson's affairs and send his furniture to Samoa.

Of all the places that Stevenson might have settled in, Samoa was one of the least likely. He and Fanny had considered Madeira; Hawaii was a possibility; Tahiti and the Marquesas were also likely. It was an American, Harry J. Moors, who welcomed Stevenson to Apia and showed him enough of the island of Upolu to interest him. Moors played a key role in getting the Stevenson's established, and he was a close friend of Stevenson's; with Fanny, however, there grew to be a coldness on both sides. Moors straightforward account gives us a view of Stevenson at the time:

"Early in December, 1889, the schooner *Equator*, with Stevenson on board, entered Apia harbor. I went aboard. A young-looking man came forward to meet me. He appeared to be about thirty years of age and somewhat sallow complexion, and about five feet ten inches in height. He wore a slight, scraggy mustache, and his hair hung down about his neck, after the fashion of artists. This was Stevenson—R.L.S., 'the best-loved initials in recent literature'—and I knew it even before he spoke. He was not a handsome man, and yet there was something irresistibly attractive about him. The genius that was in him seemed to shine out of his face. . . . He appeared to be intensely nervous, highly strung, easily excited. When I first brought him ashore

Vailima at the time the Stevensons built the house. It was later added on to by other owners and the grounds developed until it was more of an estate than a home.

he was looking somewhat weak, but hardly had he got into the street (for Apia is practically a town with but one street) when he began to walk up and down it in a most lively, not to say eccentric, manner. When I took him into my house he walked about the room, plying me with questions, one after another, darting up and down, talking on all sorts of subjects with no continuity whatever in his conversation. His wife was just as fidgety as himself, Lloyd Osbourne not much better. The long, lonesome trip on the schooner had quite unnerved them, and they were delighted to be on shore again. . . ."

"Stevenson was charmed with Samoa, and he bubbled over with delight . . . at last one day Stevenson told me he would like to make his home in Samoa permanently. 'I like this place better than any I have seen in the Pacific' . . . of all places he liked Samoa the best. 'Honolulu's good—very good,' he added, 'but this seems more savage.' "

Moors and Stevenson had some desultory conversations on the subject. Then one day he came back to Moors. He had talked it over with Fanny and she had agreed. He and Moors shook hands.

"He now asked me to look out for a nice piece of property that would suit him," wrote Moors later. "Money matters seemed to trouble him, however—not so much the first cost of the land, but the cost of the improvements that would necessarily have to follow. Finally, after several fine properties had been submitted to him for inspection, he decided that the Vailima land was the most attractive. At his request I negotiated the purchase. There were four hundred acres, and I paid $4,000."

Stevenson and Fanny in the Great Hall of Vailima. The furniture was brought from England.

And so began the last stage of Stevenson's life. His new home was financed with the help of Moors, for Stevenson, as always, lacked ready cash, even though he was now making a hundred times more money per year than any time in his life.

The land Stevenson picked—called Vailima, or Five Waters, though there were only four—lay about three miles outside of Apia, on the side of a mountain. It overlooked the town and the bay, a magnificent view, in a cool site; not far from the spot where the Stevensons planned their house was a cascading river, a waterfall and a limpid pool where they could bathe. There were three streams in all, an old native fort and another waterfall. The area they were to clear, some fifteen acres in all, lay on a kind of small plateau, below a towering mountain peak, the same peak on top of which Stevenson was someday to be buried.

While Moors took upon himself the task of clearing some of the land, the Stevensons sailed to Sydney, Australia, where Belle Strong had just had a baby. When Stevenson entered the hotel he had selected, ragged and looking like a beachcomber, he was refused a room. The party went off to a less pretentious place. But much as Sydney appealed to him, with its promise of fine foods and wines, bookstores and interesting people, Stevenson soon found himself struck down by bad health: fever, coughs, headaches, pleurisy and a severe hemorrhage. It looked as if Stevenson would die in this mildly tropical city. The only solution was to get him back to the true tropics. However, a shipping strike had tied up Sydney. Not a white sailor would move out. Finally Fanny located a small inter-island ship, owned by a Scottish firm and manned by islanders, black men and brown men. It lay outside the interests of the shipping union. On to the *Janet Nicholl* go the ravaged Stevensons, with Lloyd, and a drunken trader named Tin Jack who was recovering from his annual spree in Sydney. The ship takes a leisurely cruise through Polynesia, Micronesia and Melanesia

The "family" on the back verandah. Belle is leaning against the banister, Fanny sits directly behind Stevenson, who seems absorbed in his own thoughts. The photograph was probably taken by Lloyd.

—the heart of the South Pacific—and Stevenson regains his health. At the end of July, 1890, it returns to Sydney, and Stevenson falls ill again. What are the Stevensons to do? Writing from his sickbed in Sydney, Stevenson says to Mrs. Sitwell:

"In the South Seas, I have health, strength. I can walk and ride and be out of doors, and do my work without distress. There are great temptations, on the other hand, to go home. I do not say it is to die—because I seem incapable of dying, but I know it is to go back to the old business . . . my feeling for my friends at home has pulled me hard; but can you wonder if the hope of . . . some snatch of a man's life after all these years of the sickroom, tempted me extremely?"

So, back to Samoa they go, to the rough clearing Moors has made for them. Moors has constructed a temporary cottage—"a very neat and expensive building very like a bandstand in a German beer gar-

An afternoon ritual was the making of 'ava (or kava), a slightly hallucino-genic drink prepared from the roots of Piper mystheticum. The root might be mashed, or more properly, chewed by a young woman, expelled into the wooden bowl and mixed with water. The Stevensons left a bowl of 'ava in the Vailima smoking room for guests as a refreshing drink.

den" wrote Fanny in the diary she began keeping in September, 1890. It is rough and primitive, but the Stevensons enjoy it. A few weeks later the great Henry Adams, mourning the death of his wife with the distraction of a foreign adventure, arrives in Apia. He goes to see the Stevensons; his letters home give a good (though snobbish) por-trait of the Stevensons at home in the jungle:

"A clearing dotted with burned stumps . . . a two-story Irish shanty with steps outside to the upper floor and a galvanized iron roof . . . squalor like a railroad navvy's board hut . . . a man so thin and emaciated that he looked like a bundle of sticks in a bag, with a head and eyes morbidly intelligent and restless . . . dirty striped pajamas, the baggy legs tucked into coarse woollen stockings, one of which was bright brown in color, the other a purplish dark tone . . . a woman . . . the usual missionary nightgown which was no cleaner than her husband's shirt and drawers, but she omitted the stockings . . . complexion and eyes were dark and strong, like a half-breed Mexican." Adams adds: "Though I could not forget the dirt and discomfort, I found Stevenson extremely entertaining . . . he cannot be quiet, but sits down, jumps up, darts off and flies back, at every sentence he utters,

The Stevensons filled Vailima with rare art from Samoa and other South Pacific islands.

Stevenson and Belle work together on a manuscript. Often he dictated to Belle, for he suffered terribly from writer's cramp. "Some days we have worked from eight o'clock until four, and that is not counting the hours Louis writes and makes notes in the early morning by lamp-light. He dictates with great earnestness, and when particularly interested unconsciously acts the part of his characters." So she wrote in Memories of Vailima.

and his eyes and features gleam with a hectic glow . . . looking like an insane stork."

Square old Adams did not seem to realize that these were pioneers he was meeting, clearing land and building a new life, just as his own ancestors had hacked out their own new life in New England. Stevenson and Fanny asked Adams and his traveling companion, the artist John La Farge, to breakfast, suggesting that they might bring some of their own food since provisions were in short supply at Vailima. Mr. Adams continues with his supercilious value judgments:

"Their mode of existence is far less human than that of the natives and compared with their shanty a native house is a palace; but the squalor must be somehow due to his education. All through him, the education shows. His early associations were all second rate; he never seems by any chance to have come in contact with first-rate people, either men, women, or artists. He does not know the difference between people and mixes them up as if they were characters in his *New Arabian Nights.* Of course he must have found me out at once, for my Bostonianism, and finikin clinging to what I think the best, must rub him raw all over all the more because I try not to express it; but I suspect he does not know quite enough to hate me for it; and I am sure he would never have the finesse to penetrate La Farge, though compared with La Farge, I am a sort of Stevenson for coarseness." As for La Farge, whom Adams referred to as a person of "oriental delicacy" as opposed to the "Scotch eccentricities of Stevenson," he thought Stevenson could have spent more money on soap and less on land, and thought he was the vulgar end-product of a low rearing and of unstimulating friends. And he thought Fanny a "wild Apache."

Conditions were rought at Vailima—the road down to Apia was almost impassable, and there were at the time virtually no provisions in town. The Stevensons might lunch on a single avocado, or a can of sardines, or dine on a breadfruit. They did not think it necessary to apologize for the obvious to the pair of Bostonians.

But eventually Vailima was finished, a great house with a spreading lawn, gardens and groves of trees, a home, a showplace, a center for Stevenson's life, a life he knew might be short. A perceptive lay brother at Molokai's leper colony, who had shown Stevenson about, had picked up the feeling by instinct that Stevenson "was looking for a place wherein to end his days. . . . His objects were only suggested; but when I knew—later—who he was and more of him, these thoughts seemed more clear—that he was going to put himself away somewhere to spend his dying years."

For Stevenson, Samoa is a kind of paradise. He can do manual labor—he works in the garden, works with his hands, goes horseback

Sketch of Stevenson from Belle's notebooks.
She saw him in a romanticized light.

riding. He can live a virtually normal life. In Europe he was almost a prisoner in his sickrooms; at Skerryvore, for example, he would spend weeks indoors, going out only on rare days for a brief stroll in the garden, protected by his wife's red umbrella.

From Samoa he is to write: "For fourteen years I have not had a day's real health; I have wakened sick and gone to bed weary; and I have done my work unflinchingly. I have written in bed, and written out of it, written in hemorrhages, written in sickness, written torn by coughing, written when my head swam for weakness." But at last on this remote island, which his London-bound friends can hardly visualize and seem to resent, he can say: "I am better now, have been rightly speaking since first I came to the Pacific; and still, few are the days

A sketch of Fanny as she listens to her husband read St. Ives *aloud. The date was October 29, 1894. Stevenson was dead a few weeks later.*

when I am not in some sort of physical distress. And the battle goes on—ill or well, is a trifle."

At first the Stevensons hired some European servants, Germans mostly, but they proved to be incompetent or stupid, and gradually the household was filled with Samoans—the family, to the Stevensons. Stevenson himself became a kind of chief; he was respected and honored by the islanders. They did not understand his work, for Samoa was then in a preliterate stage. But they knew he was a great storyteller, and he was given the name of Tusitala, "the teller of stories." Each member of the family had a Samoan name or two: Fanny might be called Aolele or Flying Cloud, or Tamaitai, roughly "Madame"; there was also a less complimentary phrase for her, O le Fafine Mamana o i le Mauga, "the Witch Woman of the Mountain." Belle was Teuila, which means "she who adorns the ugly," from her habit of

Lloyd and Stevenson, with Jack, the horse. The cut-off figure at the right is that of Joe Strong. Stevenson sliced Strong out of the photograph.

The family en masse on the back verandah. Mrs. Margaret Stevenson is seated in profile, with her widow's cap. The man with the cockatoo on his shoulder is Joe Strong, whom Stevenson finally expelled from Vailima.

giving gifts to the Samoans.

Life on a grand scale continues, with visits from distinguished foreigners, visiting warships, Samoans of all ranks. And as the Stevensons become part of Samoan life, they find they are increasingly drawn into a bitter struggle between the Samoans on one side and the occupying powers—German, British, Americans—on the other. They try to be mediators, to be neutral, to be peacemakers, but the unfairness of white colonialism is apparent to Stevenson, and he begins to speak out against the colonial powers, particularly the Germans, who were especially ruthless in Samoa.

While Vailima was being settled, the Steven-
sons went off on a cruise on the Janet Nicholl.

A pact drawn up in 1889—the Treaty of Berlin, between Germany, Britain and America—tried to establish and regularize an extraterritorial, international tripartite government in Samoa, which in theory would primarily guarantee the rights of the whites and would also safeguard those of the Samoans. But the Treaty was drawn up by whites, thinking and acting as whites, and did not take into account the structure of Samoan society, with a different political system, its clans and tribes, villages, joint families and interlocking loyalties based on ties that the West no longer observed. The situation was complicated by various missionary societies, several Protestant and one Roman Catholic. The complexities grew daily as traders, government officials, missionaries shifted positions and realigned. The Germans, who had once exiled a Samoan chief named Malietota, brought him back to Apia and installed him as their puppet "king." Meanwhile, the more or less legitimate king, Mataafa, who had received some arms from the British and Americans, defeated a German landing party but was forced into hiding. Stevenson sided with Mataafa—though the British government was uneasy about him, Mataafa being a Catholic—and wrote a number of letters to the *Times* of London about the situation, exposing the chicanery of the occupying powers, no matter what nationality they were. Both the Germans and the British wanted to have him deported, but his fame was too great for an offhand action. Finally, in July, 1893, Mataafa began an armed rebellion, and the island was ravaged by the fighting. Stevenson wrote to Mark Twain:

"I wish you could see my 'simple and sunny heaven' now; war has broken out, 'they' have long been making it, 'they' have worked hard, and here it is—with its concomitants of blackened faces, severed heads and men dying in hospital." Head-taking was a common practice on both sides. "The government troops have started a horrid novelty: taking women's heads. If this leads to reprisals, we shall be a fine

An unusual photograph shows the Stevensons in their normal island dress. Here they are on Butaritari Island, during the cruise of the Janet Nicholl.

part of the world. Perhaps the best that could happen would be a complete and immediate suppression of the rebels; but, alas! all my friends (bar but a few) are in the rebellion."

Mataafa and his chiefs were defeated and exiled to the German-occupied Marshall islands. Stevenson was roundly criticized by his friends, and even by biographers, including the most recent, for "an oversimplified despair about white encroachment on and shattering of native ways." But his analysis of the situation went directly to the point:

"I can see but one way out—to follow the demand of the Samoan people that the Berlin Act be rescinded, while the three Powers withdraw absolutely, and let the natives be let alone, and allowed to govern the islands as they choose." He saw that there might be a period of internal dissension, but: "It is the patient and not the doctor who is in danger. . . . If left alone, the Samoans would continue fighting, just as they do under the tripartite treaty . . . but at least they would fight it out by themselves, without their wars being turned to the advantage of meddling foreigners."

J. C. Furnas, in his fine biography of Stevenson, then observes that "The suggestion has small realism." Actually, the two major western islands of Samoa became independent in 1960; the eastern islands —"American" Samoa—are a U.S. colony, and an example of a notoriously corrupt foreign government.

The Stevensons were a disgrace to the white race, if racial superiority is what you are trying to hold to. They weren't. Both of them went barefoot during the day, Stevenson wearing nothing but a shirt and trousers, and Fanny a great flowing Mother Hubbard and, it was rumored, nothing underneath. The Stevensons couldn't have cared less. In the evening they dressed for dinner. That was fun, too. It was their life and they lived it as they wanted to, after all those years of struggle, of poverty and not having enough to eat, of insults and rejections. Were they escaping from what they couldn't handle? I doubt it. It was physically impossible to live in a temperate climate. They lived where they would be healthy, particularly where Stevenson would be healthy. But he worked hard, nevertheless, long hours a day on a book, dictating to Belle, who lived with them (her husband finally had to be eased away; he was a drunk and a liar and ran up all sorts of bills, which he hid in a box until they were found and Stevenson paid off the creditors).

Stevenson's final work was *Weir of Hermiston*, unfinished at his death, a work that ranks high among his novels in craft and ideas. It outlines the struggle that consumed so much of his life, though he shifted the scene, the terms of the battle: the dominant father, almost monstrous in his single-mindedness, though in the book crueler, cruder than Thomas Stevenson; and the young man trying to find his way in a world where morality took second place to practicality. Ste-

*Stevenson and a local chief, Tuimalealiifono. Stevenson is in his formal
clothes, the outfit he wore for riding down to Apia on business.*

venson was too much of an artist to make the book autobiographical, but he drew heavily upon his own background, his own emotional experiences, as he needed them, to give reality to a very good work of fiction. Meanwhile other books flowed out, unceasingly, for Vailima cost him many thousands of dollars a year. Moors estimated the up-keep of the house alone at $6,500 a year, at a time when the dollar was worth many times what it is today. Stevenson's earnings at this stage probably ran to $20,000–$25,000—and were never enough. His obligations seemed to increase as his income grew. He supported a large number of people, not only Fanny and Belle and Lloyd but even directly or indirectly some of his old friends in England, a large number of Samoans and many people peripheral to his life. A generous man, who never talked of his generosity. He always was productive, but the last years were especially so, though none of the Vailima works approach the stature of a decade earlier, when he wrote *Treasure Island, The Strange Case of Dr. Jekyll and Mr. Hyde, A Child's Garden of Verses, Kidnapped* and *New Arabian Nights* within a few years of each other. But, even so, the Vailima works are worth looking into, not only *Weir of Hermiston*, but *The South Seas, The Bottle Imp, The Wrecker* (which he wrote with Lloyd), *The Beach of Falesá*, and *Island Nights' Entertainment*, to name only some of the major works.

✻

And finally the tragic moment comes, the moment the Stevensons have been fighting, have been dreading, have carried since the day they met in Grèz. This is the account in Lloyd's own words, since he was at Vailima when Stevenson died, and all the accounts draw upon his version:

"R L S was dictating some of *Weir* to my sister, and they both seemed glad to stop and listen to the budget of news I had brought up [Lloyd had just come from Apia]. I went over to the cottage to change and have a plunge in the pool. I was away perhaps an hour or

more—when I heard a curious stir in the house and a voice calling my name. Tragedy always has its own note. The intonation was sufficient to send me in startled haste across the way.

"Stevenson was lying back in an armchair, unconscious, breathing stertorously and with his unseeing eyes wide open; and on either side of him were my mother and sister, pale and apprehensive. They told me in whispers that he had suddenly cried out: 'My head—oh, my head,' and then fallen insensible. For a while we fanned him, put brandy to his lips, strove in vain to rouse him by speaking. We could not bring ourselves to believe he was dying. Then we had a cot brought down, and, taking him in my arms—it was pitiable how light he was—I carried him to it and extended him at length. By this time it was evident to us: that he had had an apoplectic stroke. His reddened face and that terrible breathing were only too conclusive."

Lloyd saddles his fastest horse and rides into Apia for a doctor. They return.

"Stevenson was still breathing in that dreadful way. The doctor looked down at him long and earnestly and then almost imperceptibly shook his head.

'A blood clot on the brain,' he said. 'He is dying.'

"In half an hour, at about eight in the evening, Stevenson was dead."

Stevenson had always wanted to be buried at the top of Mount Vaea, behind Vailima. But Lloyd had always thwarted plans to cut a path to the top of the mountain. Now it has to be done in a few hours. News of Stevenson's death spreads across Upolu, and the Samoans come to help prepare for the funeral. Before dawn they begin to cut a path up the side of the mountain:

The Samoan war was bloody and ruthless. Here, in these sketches by Belle, a war party is seen in one drawing bringing in a headless body, and in the other, offering a head to Vailima, a signal honor.

"All that morning the still air was broken by the crash of trees; the ringing sounds of axes, the hoarser thud of mattocks and crowbars on rocks. But the men themselves had been warned to make no sound; there was none of the singing and laughter that was such an inseparable part of concerted work. Silent, glistening with sweat and in a fury of effort, each strove with axe or bush knife, with mattock, spade, or pick to pay his last tribute to Tusitala. I made my way through them to the summit, my heart swelling at such determination, and chose the spot for the grave. The view from it was incomparable; the rim of the sea, risen to the height of one's eyes, gave a sense of infinite vastness; and it was all so lonely, so wild, so incredibly beautiful, that one stood there awestricken."

Meanwhile, "We washed his body and dressed it in a soft white-

Stevenson's grave atop Mount Vaea. Samoans today barely understand the reverence paid it by visiting foreigners.

linen shirt and black evening trousers girded with a dark-blue silk sash. A white tie, dark-blue silk socks and patent leather shoes completed the costume. . . . Placing the body on our big table, we drew over it the red English ensign, twelve feet long and proportionately broad, that we habitually flew over the house. Then candles were lighted." Throughout the night the Samoans had prayed beside the bier. "They were all Roman Catholics, and at intervals intoned Latin prayers in unison. There was a wonderful beauty in the cadence of that old, old tongue, so sonorous, so impressive, and so strange to hear on such lips."

While the Samoans were cutting the trail to the top of Vaea, another rite was taking place. "All that morning Stevenson's body lay in state, and in succession Chief after Chief arrived to pay his last homage. Each carried an *ie tonga*, one of those priceless old mats so finely woven that they are as soft and as pliable as a piece of silk, and which are valued in the degree of their antiquity. With an *ie tonga* in his hand each Chief advanced alone, and, stopping within a dozen feet of the body, addressed it as though it were alive. It was a touching rite, and some of the speeches were exceedingly eloquent." Lloyd speaks of one old Chief who had a "voice of magnificent range, the diction of a most accomplished orator, a power of pathos I have never heard equalled.

" 'Samoa ends with you, Tusitala,' he concluded in a peroration of tragic intensity. 'When death closed the eyes of our best and greatest friend, we knew as a race that our own day was done.' "

Then the funeral procession begins. "At two o'clock the coffin was brought out by a dozen powerful Samoans, who led the way with it up the mountain. Directly behind were thirty or forty more men, who at intervals changed places with the bearers. It was a point of honor with them all to keep their heavy burden shoulder-high, though how they contrived to do so on that precipitous path was a seeming impossibility. . . .

"We gathered about the grave, and no cathedral could have seemed nobler or more hallowed than the grandeur of nature that encompassed us. What fabric of men's hands could vie with such solitude? The sea in front, the primeval forest behind, crags, precipices, and distant cataracts gleaming in an untrodden wilderness. The words of the Church of England service, movingly delivered, broke the silence in which we stood. The coffin was lowered; flowers strewn on it, and then the hurrying spades began to throw back the earth."

❋

And then they began to rewrite the past.

Cummy lived to the age of ninety-two, dying in 1910, always cherishing Stevenson's memory.

A FOOTNOTE TO HISTORY

Here he lies where he longed to be;
Home is the sailor, home from the sea,
And the hunter home from the hill.

SO, the last lines of his "Requiem," which he wrote out in a rough draft as he lay close to death under the fragrant pines in the California mountains, fearful of losing Mrs. Osbourne. Not great poetry, is it? A bit on the square side, in fact. But a fitting epitaph for that great wanderer, Captain George North, seaman and adventurer, the seeker of new horizons, who had sailed off into the savage South Seas. For it has been the Captain I have been writing about, the daring adventurer disguised as a frail, blood-coughing Scottish writer, a scribbler, failed engineer, unsuccessful lawyer. "Requiem" adorns the undistinguished cement tomb that covers the Captain's grave atop Mount Vaea. An absolutely fantastic view from the tiny plateau atop the mountain. No man could ask for a more beautiful resting place for his bones. Three miles down from Vailima, which one can see nesting

140

Lloyd Osbourne, making the most of the fame and fortune inherited from his long association with Stevenson, took up a life of serious pleasure. Something of a cad about him, one suspects.

far below the tomb, is the town of Apia, not much larger than when Harry Moors greeted the Stevensons as they come ashore from the *Equator*.

The great house is still standing, having survived various vicissitudes. Fanny tried to live there after her husband's death but found that it was not feasible without him. A German trader bought it from her for $10,000, Moors having served as middleman. Canny chap,

*After her husband's death, Fanny Stevenson struck off on the diffi-
cult role of being not only the widow of a famous man, but an
individual in her own right. She was energetic, dynamic, outspoken.*

Moors. When World War I came, the New Zealanders ousted the
Germans. The house served for a while as the governor's mansion.
When I visited it in the 1970's it was empty and locked, guarded by a
bored Samoan policeman. The man who had the key was "away."

Fanny returned to the States, a respected, powerful woman, the
widow of a great man. But a person in her own right, no doubt about

*Belle (weeping) and Fanny gaze at the San Fran-
cisco skyline as they set off on one of their cruises.*

Dressed in the abominable black of the aged that fashion once demanded, Fanny is seen in one of the last photographs before her death. But her glance is still sharp, the piercing gaze that Stevenson once compared to the "sighting of a pistol."

that. Something of a character, too. At the age of sixty-four she aquired a young secretary, Edward Salisbury Field, then aged twenty-four. They traveled together a lot, lived in several different houses. Much speculation on their relationship ("but he's young enough to be her son!"). Six months after Fanny died (the date was February 18, 1914), Ned Field married her daughter Belle, a mere fifty-four and long-since divorced from the erratic Joe Strong. The next year they took Fanny's ashes to Upolu and buried them next to Stevenson on Mount Vaea. Fielding was something of a writer, though not a great one (lightweight plays: *Good Intentions, Twin Beds, The Rented Earl,* the highly successful *Wedding Bells;* he also did the film version of *Little Women* that starred Katharine Hepburn). He dabbled in California real estate and became rich when oil was discovered on his land. Lloyd, who shared in the Stevenson royalties, became an auto freak, wrote a book called *The Motormaniacs,* along with some nice reminiscences of his stepfather, married and divorced a dull, angry young woman named Katharine Durham, and became a playboy like his father. Now they are all gone, Ned Field dying in 1936; Lloyd in 1947; and Nellie in 1953, aged ninety-five.

*

> Glad did I live and gladly die,
> And laid me down with a will.

It was a hard life but a good one.